BRANDS

Marcel Danesi's outstanding introduction traces the origins and development of brands and brand identity, posing the question, "Why does giving names to common products transform them into meaningful objects?" From Coca-Cola to Coco Chanel, Gucci to Guinness, Marcel Danesi tackles the topic of brands from the perspective of semiotics—the science that studies the "psychology of signs" in cultural settings.

Brands explores:

- from product to brand: advertising and brands, the naming of products, brands as mental constructs and signification systems
- brand textuality: textuality, language and visual devices and meta-textuality
- the branding of culture
- brand globalization.

Marcel Danesi is Professor of Anthropology and Semiotics at the University of Toronto and Fellow of the Royal Society of Canada. He is also Director of the Program in Semiotics and Communication Theory at the University of Toronto. Since 2004 he has been Editor-in-Chief of the journal *Semiotica*.

ROUTLEDGE INTRODUCTIONS TO MEDIA AND COMMUNICATIONS

Edited by Paul Cobley *London Metropolitan University*

This new series provides concise introductions to key areas in contemporary communications. Each book in the series addresses a genre or a form of communication, analysing the nature of the genre or the form as well as reviewing its production and consumption, outlining the main theories and approaches that have been used to study it, and discussing contemporary textual examples of the form. The series offers both an outline of how each genre or form has developed historically, and how it is changing and adapting to the contemporary media landscape, exploring issues such as convergence and globalization.

Videogames
James Newman

Brands
Marcel Danesi

Advertising
Ian MacRury

Magazines
Anna Gough-Yates

Youth Media
Bill Osgerby

News
Jackie Harrison

Cyberspace
Mike Ledgerwood

Internet
Lorenzo Cantoni and Stefano Tardini

BRANDS

Marcel Danesi

2006

Routledge
Taylor & Francis Group

NEW YORK AND LONDON

First published 2006
by Taylor & Francis Inc.
270 Madison Ave, New York, NY 10016

Simultaneously published in the UK
by Routledge
2 Park Square, Milton Park, Abingdon, Oxon OX14 4RN

*Routledge is an imprint of the Taylor & Francis Group,
an informa business*

© 2006 Marcel Danesi

Typeset in Perpetua and Univers by
Florence Production Ltd, Stoodleigh, Devon
Printed and bound in Great Britain by
TJ International Ltd, Padstow, Cornwall

British Library Cataloguing in Publication Data
A catalogue record for this book is available from
the British Library

Library of Congress Cataloging in Publication Data
A catalog record for this book has been requested

ISBN10: 0–415–27997–6 (hbk)
ISBN10: 0–415–27998–4 (pbk)
ISBN10: 0–203–64249–X (ebk)

ISBN13: 978–0–415–27997–0 (hbk)
ISBN13: 978–0–415–27998–7 (pbk)
ISBN13: 978–0–203–64249–8 (ebk)

CONTENTS

ILLUSTRATIONS

FIGURES

TABLES

SERIES EDITOR'S PREFACE

There can be no doubt that communications pervade contemporary social life. The audio-visual media, print, and other communication technologies play major parts in modern human existence, mediating diverse interactions between people. Moreover, they are numerous, heterogeneous, and multi-faceted.

Equally, there can be no doubt that communications are dynamic and ever-changing, constantly reacting to economic and popular forces. Communicative genres and modes that we take for granted because they are seemingly omnipresent—news, advertising, film, radio, television, fashion, the book—have undergone alarming sea changes in recent years. They have also been supplemented and reinvigorated by new media, new textualities, new relations of production, and new audiences.

The *study* of communications, then, cannot afford to stand still. Although communications study as a discipline is relatively recent in its origin, it has continued to develop in recognizable ways, embracing new perspectives, transforming old ones, and responding to—and sometimes influencing—changes in the media landscape.

This series of books is designed to present developments in contemporary media. It focuses on the analysis of textualities, offering an up-to-date assessment of current communications practice. The emphasis of the books is on the *kind* of communications which constitute the modern media and the theoretical tools which are needed to understand them. Such tools may include semiotics (including social semiotics and semiology), discourse theory, poststructuralism, postcolonialism, queer theory, gender analysis, political economy, liberal pluralism, positivism (including quantitative approaches), qualitative methodologies (including the "new ethnography"), reception theory, and ideological analysis. The breadth of current communications media, then, is reflected in the array of methodological resources needed to investigate them.

Yet the task of analysis is not carried out as a hermetic experiment. Each volume in the series places its topic within a contextual matrix of production and consumption. Each allows readers to garner an understanding of what that communication is like without tempting them to forget who produced it, for what purpose, and with what result. The books seek to present research on the mechanisms of textuality but also attempt to reveal the precise situation in which such mechanisms exist. Readers coming to these books will therefore gain a valuable insight into the present standing of specific communications media. Just as importantly, though, they will become acquainted with analytic methods which address, explore, and interrogate the very bases of that standing.

ACKNOWLEDGMENTS

I must thank Victoria College of the University of Toronto for having allowed me the privilege of teaching and coordinating its Program in Semiotics and Communication Theory over many years. I must also thank my wonderful students at both the University of Toronto and the University of Lugano who, over the last few years, have been involved in collecting information on my behalf for the purposes of this book. Indeed, most of the original findings reported here are a result of what will be called the "Toronto–Lugano research team." This consisted of eight students who collected data, interviewed people, and found relevant information in those two cities that will be reported in this book.

I would also like to express my sincere gratitude to the many colleagues who have given me their precious input over the years, both at professional conferences and through correspondence. I am especially grateful to Paul Cobley, not only for inviting me to contribute to this Routledge series, but also for providing me with truly insightful suggestions on how to improve my treatment. His own work, moreover, has been a genuine source of inspiration. I must also thank Naomi Klein, author of *No Logo* (a book that has been instrumental in raising awareness on the dangers posed by the spread of brand culture) for her support and encouragement, even though there are a number of points of difference between our individual interpretations of the branding phenomenon. Last, but not least, I must pay homage to the late Professor Thomas A. Sebeok. I dedicate this book to his memory. Now that he is no longer among us, I have come to realize what a truly humane person he was. What the German philosopher Arthur Schopenhauer

(1788–1860) wrote about great thinkers certainly applies to Tom Sebeok: "Great minds are related to the brief span of time during which they live as great buildings are to a little square in which they stand: you cannot see them in all their magnitude because you are standing too close to them."

Marcel Danesi
University of Toronto, 2005

INTRODUCTION

The practice of giving "brand names" to common household products originated near the end of the nineteenth century, when a small group of manufacturers adopted it in the belief that it would give their products an edge in the ever-expanding and highly competitive free-market economy system. Common folk, they thought, would remember and recognize their products if they had a name and, thus, be more inclined to acquire them over competing nameless products. The strategy worked beyond their expectations, generating significant profits for commodity producers. At the turn of the twentieth century, manufacturer after manufacturer jumped on the brand-naming bandwagon. By the 1920s, the strategy led to a widespread perception of brand products as "signs" imbued with specific kinds of personal and lifestyle meanings.

The question of why the naming of products has engendered this perception is, in my view, a critical one for understanding modern-day consumer behavior and communal "groupthink." Why does giving brand names to toothpastes, soap bars, pens, automobiles, or lipsticks transform them into signs of personality and lifestyle? This book will attempt to answer this question from the perspective of *semiotics*—the science that studies the "psychology of signs" in cultural settings. Naming a product is, *tout court,* a "semiotic act." But, most importantly, semiotic acts involve not only the possibility of designation or denotation; they also facilitate the conjuring of associations.

This book is intended mainly as a practical guide on how this seemingly simple act has brought about the branding of culture. Since my treatment is intended to reach a broad audience, I have made no technical assumptions whatsoever, defining and illustrating each semiotic concept practically and concretely. I have also avoided making constant references to the technical literature. The works that have informed my commentaries, descriptions, and analyses are listed in the Further Reading section on pp. 147–51.

I have tried to cast as wide a net as possible, attempting to exemplify within two covers how semiotics can be used effectively to probe social trends in specific ways. I also wish to assure the reader that I have made every attempt possible to emphasize method of analysis, rather than my personal views. Since I live and teach in Canada, I have taken most of the illustrations and examples for discussion and analysis from North American consumerist culture. However, since many of these have become part of the "global marketplace," I am confident that they will be recognized virtually anywhere in the world today. Indeed, Chapter 6 suggests that this is an integral feature of contemporary brands: that they have become globalized.

Before proceeding, however, it is worth getting straight what we mean when we talk about brands and branding. This might seem like a simple matter. In the modern world, consumers have become used to asking for, and recognizing, by their brand names, those things they buy. Yet it is important to the analysis of brands to avoid slippage between what is the brand and what is the "product," as well as to recognize that products have lives as goods or commodities. Let us start with the product first. A 2-inch square of wire wool with some detergent stuck to it is a product. It has a chemical composition and a shape in the world. These are the features that tend to define it and which are certainly most apparent when we encounter it. However, if that product—some "thing" that has been *produced*—is the subject of a further interaction, its use value becomes clearer. It may, for example, be utilized in the cleaning of particularly heavily stained pans, especially in combination with hot water. As such, it has become a commodity or a "good" (the latter more commonly used when referring to commodities in the plural: "goods").

When a product becomes a commodity or a good, it takes on some use value for someone. Yet, given the fact that a product is *produced*, there is a sense in which it is already disposed to become something useful. As such, the movement from a product to a commodity is swift and largely imperceptible. This is why there tends to be a distinction in the minds of most people between the *product* and the *brand* (rather than a distinction of product, commodity and brand). What is most important, however, is that the use value of a product-commodity makes it especially amenable to associations from its human users. This was something that Marx recognized about commodities immediately in *Das Kapital*. It is also what makes branding seem so "natural."

When a product-commodity becomes a brand, its use value is supplemented by a number of further associations. The detergent-infused wire-wool square, when called "Brillo" and packaged in a characteristic style, becomes susceptible to the kind of associations that will be analyzed throughout this book. Indeed, it is even possible that those associations will be so strong that they elevate Brillo to the position where it is synonymous with pan-scouring pads in general and, possibly, the pinnacle of quality in relation to such commodities. The position of the Brillo brand, of course, will be attained and sustained by more than just its name. As mentioned, the packaging will be crucial; as will a series of discourses surrounding the brand. These will include the descriptions that appear on the package and word-of-mouth recommendations among consumers. Most importantly, perhaps, they will also involve the massive work of advertising, a discourse that raises brand awareness.

As I will argue in this book, brands are ubiquitous: we have a branded culture in the West and brands are disseminated across the globe. Brands are one of the most important modes of communication in the modern media environment. In fact, it seems that there is no place where branding is not taking place. A supermarket's own commodities are sometimes thought of as if they were *not* brands. Safeway's own, "unbranded," peanut butter seems to have no brand at all. However, it takes just a little thought to realize that Safeway peanut butter is precisely branded as "Safeway's." Supermarket own-brands are certainly subject to less financial investment than other, bigger brands—they are seldom specifically advertised, for example. However, they are still brands in their own right. In UK supermarkets, for instance, this is recognized by consumers and producers alike through the process of "internal" branding: both Tesco's and Sainsbury's supermarkets have their own, demarcated upmarket food brands ("Finest" and "Taste the Difference," respectively) which are differentiated from the other own-brand food offered in those stores. These are almost brands within brands. Furthermore, consumers may even recognize the "brand behind no brand": the bread in the food section of UK branches of the Europe-wide traditional store, Marks & Spencer, is well known to be produced by Rank Hovis McDougall.

In considering the ubiquity of brands, it is worth keeping in mind the semiotic nature of the movement through product-commodity to brand. Undoubtedly, it is a movement that involves the expansion of associations that accrue to an item, featuring no perception of something, followed by increasing knowledge of something, culminating in an immersion in the imputed sign function of that something. As such, it is analogous to the important distinction between "thing," "object," and "sign" in semiotics as discussed so cogently by the American philosopher, John Deely (1994: 11–22). It should be clear throughout what follows that the generating of associations that is stimulated by brands is absolutely central to understanding what a brand (in its sign function) is.

Chapter 2, therefore, begins with questions of brand identity. What is it? How is it produced? What is the semiotic act that transforms products into mental phenomena? The chapter shows how brands and advertising are inextricably intertwined and demonstrates the importance of the vagaries of naming practices. Chapter 3 deals with brand image or, to put the matter another way, deals with the strategies of the brand managers. Naming is one of them, but Chapter 3 then goes on to discuss logos and product/container design, and the relating of advertising texts to the foregoing brand mix. In order to carry out the analysis, the semiotic processes of connotation and denotation are recapitulated from Chapter 2.

Where Chapter 3 deals with brand image, Chapter 4 deals with brand textuality. It is true, of course, that images are as much "texts" as writing is; but the chapter is particularly concerned with linguistically based slogans and jingles, and how these interact with themes, characters, and images. Specifically, Chapter 4 is concerned with how a "text" is created. Chapter 5 extends the principle of general textuality to look at the way in which the "branding of culture" takes place. The argument that the texts of brand management and those of other cultural sectors are coextensive or no longer perceived as different is considered. It extends the concerns of Chapter 4 by looking, in particular, at advertising campaigns, and the linguistic and pictorial means that have been used to sustain them.

Chapter 6 explores what might be the logical conclusion of the branding of culture in the West: the globalization of brands. It proceeds from McLuhan's prediction that we will be increasingly living in a "Global Village" (1964: 23) rather than a planet characterized by long distances between different cultures. The chapter will therefore discuss the argument that the community entailed by the Global Village is dominated by brands and the techniques of brand management. That this scenario is so plausible and so prevalent is demonstrated by the fact that there is a significant "anti-branding" movement (connected to the nebulous anti-globalization movement); this is discussed in the later part of the chapter.

In general, this book will be an attempt to show how brands are signs that represent ideas that have strong emotional appeal. What is needed to understand brands is a means of investigating these signs. In order to do this, an explanatory semiotic theory is required. What follows, then, is an attempt to explain brands using such a theory and to offer people a means to become aware of the image-making strategies that are utilized to promote unbridled materialism.

2

FROM PRODUCT
TO BRAND

> My image is a statement of the symbols of the harsh, impersonal prod-
> ucts and brash materialistic objects on which America is built today. It is
> a projection of everything that can be bought and sold, the practical but
> impermanent symbols that sustain us.
>
> Andy Warhol (1928–87)

Today, companies invest considerable time and resources into creating
appropriate "brand identities" for themselves—identities that generate a
sense of goodwill and care for the product. It is no exaggeration to claim
that economic stability and even survival depend on carving out such
identities. As Bedbury has aptly put it:

> It can safely be said that Coca-Cola's total market value is more an emotional
> quantity than a physical one. Hard assets like bottling plants, trucks, raw
> materials, and buildings are not as important to Coke—or Wall Street, for
> that matter—as the consumer goodwill that exists around the world toward
> the brand.
>
> (Bedbury 2002: 12)

How does one create brand identity, spread it, and sustain it in an
ever-changing world? Answers to this question are the directives that
motivate marketing science today—a science that is taking on, more
and more, the look of a semiotic science in how it now tends to put the
role of "signifying structures" of human psychology at the center of its

methodology using, like semiotics, an interdisciplinary blends of psychology, statistics, anthropology, and sociology in an approach that mirrors the multifaceted nature of the brand phenomenon. Marketers are finally beginning to perceive brands as signs that link products and users within an overarching system of meanings that we call a culture.

Originally, the term "branding" referred to the searing of flesh with a hot iron to produce a scar or mark with an easily recognizable pattern for identification purposes. Livestock were branded by the Egyptians as early as 2000 BCE. This practice was brought to North America in the sixteenth century by the Spanish conqueror Hernán Cortés (1485–1547). Used primarily as proof of ownership, branding developed over time into a practice for keeping records on quality. In most American cattle states, the law requires the registration of brands, and altering a brand is a criminal offense. Branding has also been used on human beings—the branding of prisoners, for instance, was a form of punishment used by the ancient Greeks and Romans, and was later adopted by the Anglo-Saxons. Criminals, slaves, army deserters, and "sinners" (such as women alleged to be witches) have been branded in the past. The practice declined around the middle of the nineteenth century.

The goal of this opening chapter is to unravel the roots of branding as a semiotic act that transforms products into mental phenomena. As Alina Wheeler has observed: "Products are created in the factory; brands are created in the mind" (2003: 2). At what point in time, and for what reasons, did products become brands? One simple mechanism cannot be responsible; it must be a matter of a number of different semiotic strategies. No doubt, without modern-day advertising, this transformation would never have occurred. The histories of advertising and branding are inextricably intertwined. Thus, the point of departure for probing this transformation is an examination of the relation between advertising and brands.

ADVERTISING AND BRANDS

The term "advertising" comes from the medieval Latin verb *advertere*, "to direct one's attention to." Originally, it referred to any type or form of public announcement intended to direct people's attention to the availability, qualities, and cost of specific commodities or services. With few exceptions—e.g. the classified ads in a newspaper—this is hardly what is meant by this term today. Today, advertising is more an art of persuasion than it is of information, designed to showcase a product in the marketplace in terms of how it can satisfy various emotional, social, and other kinds of human needs.

Given its pervasiveness, it should come as little surprise to find studies claiming that advertising has influenced social "groupthink" in a profound way. "Groupthink" is the term used by social scientists to designate the set of assumed ideas, values, beliefs, and lifestyle modes that are shared by a group of people living in the same, or similar, social framework based on a shared culture. Sales pitches for products fill the pages of newspapers and magazines; they are spread through posters on buses, subways, trains, city walls, etc. Neon signs flash them throughout cities and on billboards along the roadsides. Commercials interrupt TV and radio programs, enticing us to buy products. In a phrase, the images of advertisers have become part of the social landscape, influencing what we perceive to have value in personal and social terms. This is no doubt why advertising has been adopted since at least the 1950s by politicians, social activists, health institutions, and virtually anyone who wishes to gain the attention of different publics and to promote their perspectives or causes. Pressure groups of various kinds have even taken to the practice of "branding" themselves, so as to make it easy for people to recognize instantly their cause, be it anti-smoking, anti-drug, etc. Politicians at all levels of government now communicate their platforms and their personal perspectives on social issues regularly through sleek ad campaigns, with appurtenant slogans and other techniques deployed by the world of business. The modern world has become one large "mega-advertising" universe in which dreams and aspirations are filtered through the images of the advertiser's camera. As the social commentator E. B. White put it:

> Advertisers are the interpreters of our dreams—Joseph interpreting for Pharaoh. Like the movies, they infect the routine futility of our days with purposeful adventure. Their weapons are our weaknesses: fear, ambition, illness, pride, selfishness, desire, and ignorance. And these weapons must be kept as bright as a sword.
>
> (White 1991: 36)

Modern-day advertising is an art form that has forged a partnership with marketing science, with the latter conducting extensive ethnographic and quantitative surveys to help assess the likely efficacy of specific advertising campaigns before they are mounted. Like anthropologists and semioticians, marketers observe people in their ambiances as they react to ads and to branded messages.

Advertising has thus become a widespread type of persuasive discourse that is now employed by anyone wishing to make public statements.

It is the new grammar of propaganda, publicity, and public-relations domains. What we mean by this can be broken down into the following. Propaganda is the craft of spreading and entrenching doctrines, views, and beliefs, reflecting specific interests and ideologies (political, social, philosophical, etc.) by attempting to persuade people through emotional appeals. Publicity is the business of disseminating any information that concerns a particular stakeholder (a person, a group, etc.) through some public medium, so as to garner attention for the stakeholder. Public relations (PR) is the art that aims to establish favorable attitudes and responses towards organizations, institutions, and individuals. Advertising serves the goals of these enterprises perfectly because its aim, like that of a work of fiction, is to appeal to the lingering after-effects in the individual's mind. As such, it differs from, say, the goal of philosophical or scientific discourse, that respectively leave people in a pugnacious or pensive mood. It deals not so much with rational thought processes, but with the residues of emotions that pervade thought.

The increasing success of brand advertising in promoting the sales of specific goods and services gave birth in 1914 to the *Audit Bureau of Circulations* in the US, an independent organization founded and supported by newspaper and magazine publishers who wanted to obtain circulation statistics and to standardize the ways of presenting them. In 1936, the *Advertising Research Foundation* was established to conduct research on the effectiveness of different advertising techniques. Today, the increasing sophistication of statistical information-gathering and data-processing techniques makes it possible for many brands to direct their advertising campaigns towards specific "market segments"—i.e. groups of people classified on the basis of where they live, what income they make, what educational backgrounds they have, etc.—in order to determine their susceptibility to, or inclination towards, their identities.

While the concept of brand as a name assigned to a product is not more than 150 years old, the practice of differentiating products and services by some symbolic technique is actually very old. The trademark, for instance, is any visual symbol that identifies a product or service; it has existed since the dawn of history. Archaeologists have discovered outdoor signs with trademarks displayed on them above the shop doors of ancient cities of the Middle East. The ancient Greeks and Romans hung similar signs outside their shops. Trademarks were used because most of the population was not literate. Trademarks were such that they could be deciphered by anyone, literate or not. They were intended, literally, as "marks" of the "trade" so that people could easily identify specific products or services, and distinguish them from those made or sold by others. Among the best-known trademarks surviving from the medieval period, for example, are the striped pole of the barbershop and the three-ball sign of the pawnbroker shop. Some products, such as swords and pottery, were also marked with identifiable visual marks so that buyers could trace their origin and determine their quality.

Likewise, it should not be imagined that the advertising of goods is solely a product of the modern world. The practice of announcing the availability of goods and services was a common one in ancient Egypt, for instance, where merchants hired "criers" to walk through the streets broadcasting the arrival of ships and their cargo at the top of their voices. Many outdoor posters and mural inscriptions also contained advertising messages. One of the oldest posters was found among the ruins of ancient Rome. It offered property for rent. Another early "ad" found painted on a wall in Pompeii calls the attention of travelers to a tavern located in a different town. Throughout the ancient world, poster and picture ads in marketplaces and temples seem to have constituted a means of disseminating information and of promoting the barter and sale of goods and services.

Such practices continued uninterrupted right into the medieval period. Their reach was, however, limited. All this changed with the invention of the modern printing press by Johann Gutenberg (c. 1400–68), which introduced the kind of technology that was needed for mass advertising to become practicable. Fliers and posters could be printed quickly and cheaply, and put in many public places or inserted in books, pamphlets, and newspapers. By the seventeenth century, print advertising was fast becoming an intrinsic part of the "Gutenberg Galaxy," as the Canadian communications theorist Marshall McLuhan (1911–80) characterized the new (and shrinking) world that ensued from the spread of print technology (McLuhan 1962). The *London Gazette* became the first newspaper to reserve a section exclusively for advertising. So successful was this venture that, by the end of the century, several agencies came into existence for the specific purpose of creating newspaper ads for merchants and artisans in Britain. The ads were more like modern classifieds, without illustrative support, than they were persuasive rhetorical texts. But they clearly anticipated some of the rhetorical techniques of their contemporary descendants. The ad makers of the era catered to wealthy clients who bought and read newspapers. They were designed to promote the sale of such high-society products as tea, coffee, wigs, books, theater tickets, and the like. The following advertisement for toothpaste was published in the *Gazette* in 1660. Its rhetorical slant clearly foreshadows the kind of persuasive style used today for the promotion of this type of product:

> Most excellent and proved Dentifrice to scour and cleanse the Teeth, making them white as ivory, preserves the Tooth-ach; so that being constantly used, the Parties using it are never troubled with the Tooth-ach. It fastens the Teeth, sweetens the Breath, and preserves the Gums and Mouth from cankers and Impothumes, and the right are only to be had at Thomas Rookes, Stationer.
>
> (Cited by Dyer 1982: 16–17)

Note that the creator of the ad describes the dentifrice as being "excellent" and "proved," implying that scientific testing has been conducted on the product. For this reason, the product should allow its users to make their teeth "white as ivory" and to overcome toothache, cankers, and other buccal maladies. Most significantly, the ad suggests, by innuendo, that the toothpaste will enhance the social life of its users for the reason that it also "sweetens the Breath." By the eighteenth century, this rhetorical style of advertising had become so commonplace that lexicographer Samuel Johnson (1709–84) felt impelled to write the following discerning appraisal in *The Idler*: "Advertisements are now so numerous that they are very negligently perused, and it is therefore become necessary to gain attention by magnificence of promise and by eloquence sometimes sublime and sometimes pathetic" (cited by Panati 1984: 168).

With the advent of industrialization in the nineteenth century, rhetorical advertising took on an increasingly important role as a means for manufacturers to coax people into buying their products in an increasingly competitive marketplace. Ad layouts were created more and more to be eye-catching. The words were set out in attractive fonts; compact sentences were employed to make a pitch sound more informal, colloquial, humorous, and personal; illustrations were added to emphasize the ad's message visually. Advertising copy was being designed more and more, as Dyer notes, "to attract attention to a product" (1982: 32). Advertising was slowly evolving into an art of persuasion, surreptitiously starting even to influence everyday discourse, as more and more people became exposed to ad messages in newspapers, magazines, and on posters, using the particular phraseology of ad slogans to refer to all kinds of topics. Advertising in the early stages of the modern industrialized world, then, was already ripe for the kinds of strategies that brand management demanded—principally, the emphasis on the associations of the product advertised.

NAMING PRODUCTS

The stage was set by the middle part of the nineteenth century for consumer products to evolve into much more than objects, culminating in the 1880s with the radical new strategy on the part of a few manufacturers of assigning names to products. It is not known which product was named first, but the 1882 naming by Harley Proctor of his generically named "White Soap" as "Ivory Soap"—an idea that apparently came to him while reading a psalm in church—is considered to be the most likely candidate by most historiographers of advertising. In December of that year, Proctor also introduced the slogan into advertising, referring to Ivory Soap in all his promotional literature as "99 and 44/100% pure." As Proctor realized, a slogan is effective as a memory-aiding device because it is an elaboration of the brand name—a kind of self-styled definition of it. The concept of brand was thus born. There were many soap products, but there was only one, named Ivory, that was "99 and 44/100% pure." Ivory thus became a unique type of soap, not just any other soap. By simply labeling products in grocery, dry goods, and department stores with descriptive or colorful names, manufacturers soon found that sales of the products increased significantly. In some cases, the trademark was used as the brand name for the product. Such was the case with the Parker Pen Company—one of the first trademarks to be converted into a brand name in 1888 in Janesville, Wisconsin, by George Safford Parker. Parker simply named each pen produced by his a company a "Parker pen." The strategy worked brilliantly—the Parker Pen Company became the world's largest producer of fountain pens in the latter part of the nineteenth century.

In Britain as well, the brand-named product had come into being by the end of the nineteenth century. It was the food industry in that country that provided the first brands with names such as Bovril, Hovis, Nestlé, Cadbury, Fry, and Kellogg. The brand name was then assigned to products of new technologies, such as the sewing machine, camera, bicycle, and typewriter. By the 1920s, brands became the focus of advertising, linking the brand to a particular image, both rhetorical and visual. The course of consumerist society changed drastically and has never been the same since.

Why would the act of naming products change the course of consumerist society? The answer to this question is, basically, the goal of this book. For the present purposes, suffice it to say that the naming act itself is semiotically powerful. Across cultures, names are perceived as fundamental to the identification and personality of the individual. Without a name, a human being is often taken to have no true existence psychologically and socially. Names are "life-givers" in psychological terms. By naming a product, the manufacturer is, in effect, bestowing upon it the same kinds of meanings that are reserved for people. In a basic psychological sense, a product that is named is "humanized."

The naming of goods and services went into full swing in the 1880s and 1890s, as firms began to market everyday household products that were previously sold in neighborhood stores randomly from large bulk containers as brands. The sales of products named Pears', Sapolio, Colgate, Kirk's American Family, Royal Baking Powder, Quaker Oats, Baker's Chocolate, Hire's Root Beer, Regal Shoes, Parker Pens, Bon Ami, Wrigley, and Coca-Cola (to mention a few) increased noticeably as people started asking for them by name. By the end of the century, the concept of brands had become part and parcel of a changing market-place—a marketplace that was becoming increasingly aware of the power of symbolism in human psychology.

Above all else, naming a product makes it possible to refer to it as if it had a distinctive character or quality—"I don't trust Colgate products; they're useless"; "I will only buy Quaker's; it suits me perfectly"; etc. It is meaningless to say something like "I don't trust the toothpaste that has blue stripes in it"; or "I will buy only the cereal that has an oat-like taste to it." Moreover, a product with a name has the capacity, as a lexical item, to tap into the brain's memory reservoir. It is easier to remember things as words than to remember the things themselves. A word classifies something, keeps it distinct from other things, and, above all else, bestows socially relevant meanings to it. The name Ivory, for example, evokes an image of something "ultra-white"; Royal Baking Powder of something "regal" and "splendid"; Bon Ami of "a good friend," and so on. Such suggestive images stick in the mind, in the same way that the meanings of ordinary words do. They become a part of our semantic memory system.

Because of this semantic and cultural dimension of naming, it comes as little surprise to find that the term "brand" is no longer used today just to refer to a specific product line, but also to the company that manu-factures it and to the social image that the company wishes to impart of itself and of its products. Thus, the name Coca-Cola now refers not only to the actual soft drink, but also to the company itself, the social meanings that drinking coke entails, etc. The drink was subsequently promoted with such slogans as "Wonderful nerve and brain tonic and remarkable therapeutic agent" and "Its beneficial effects upon diseases of the vocal cords are wonderful." In 1891, Atlanta pharmacist Asa G. Candler acquired ownership of Coca-Cola, changing its image from a "brain tonic" to that of a popular 5¢ soft drink that could be drunk together with family and friends—an image that has persisted to this day and is the basis of Coca-Cola's continued commercial success.

That image was created at first by imprinting the Coca-Cola name/logo on drinking glasses, providing them to diners and other eateries that featured "pop" and foods meant to be eaten quickly and cheaply. Coca-Cola became a fountain drink and eventually a bottled drink, delivered by truck to hard-to-reach places (Hays 2004). Since then, Coca-Cola has become a brand that is sometimes closely associated with socially relevant themes, as can be witnessed in its brotherly love and peace ad campaign during the counterculture era of the late 1960s and early 1970s with its "I'd like to teach the world to sing in perfect harmony" jingle that became a hit song on its own.

Coca-Cola was also one of the first brands to carve out for itself a "brand image," as it has come to be known. This can be defined as the opinion or concept of the product that is held by the public, especially as filtered through the mass media. By 1900, advertising campaigns designed to promote brand image were becoming the norm. In tandem, consumption increased and corporations grew into mammoth structures that transformed the workplace into an integrated economic system of mass production. From the 1920s onwards, advertising and public relations agencies flourished, developing increasingly sophisticated image-making techniques for building a bridge between brands and consumer perception. Everything from brand name, design, and packaging came gradually within the purview of this new "image-making" business sector. Business and psychology had joined forces once and for all in the new marketplace.

The advent of radio in the 1920s gave the brands a new channel to spread their imagery—the radio commercial message which was a mini-narrative that revolved around a brand and its socially relevant functions. Since radio reached masses of people, print literate or not, radio commercials, which often included catchy tunes called "jingles," became highly influential as techniques for disseminating brand imagery throughout society. With the advent of television in the late 1940s, the commercial was adapted to the new visual medium. For example, Folger's Coffee commercials, with their pseudoscientific sales pitches in which statements were made using the style of scientific language ("proven," "shown to be," "by most people," etc.), Mum Deodorant commercials, which were satires of spy movies, and Pepsodent Toothpaste commercials with their snappy jingles, were given a visual and thus more effective modality by the new medium. As households across North

America started to acquire a TV set, such products became so familiar that perception of the brand became inextricably intertwined with the style and content of the commercials created to promote it.

It was clear from the outset that the medium of television had great persuasive power, and the brands exploited this fully. TV toy commercials, for instance, started the trend of inducing parents to believe that certain toys had educational value. Commercials designed to sell insurance, fire alarms, cosmetics, and vitamin capsules were designed to evoke fear (of sickness, crime, loss of social standing, impending disaster, etc.). TV gave visual form to fictitious radio cartoon characters—such as Mr Clean, a brawny and bald "dirt fighter," and Speedy, a personified tablet who represented the Alka-Seltzer brand of antacid tablet. TV also helped to spread brand imagery by the use of jingles, such as the "Mr Clean in a just a minute" jingle (for the Mr Clean detergent product) and the "Plop, plop, fizz, fizz, oh what a relief it is" jingle (for the Alka-Seltzer stomach pain relief product).

By the mid-1960s, the boundaries between TV programming in the US and the brands that sponsored them became increasingly blurred. Advertising agencies produced nearly all network programming. Stations often sold agencies full sponsorship, which included placing a product name in a show's title—e.g. The Texaco Theater. The ratings system used in broadcasting arose, in fact, from the sponsors' desire to know how many people they were reaching with their "brand placement" strategies. The A. C. Nielsen Company, which had been surveying audience size in radio since the mid-1930s in the US, eventually became the dominant TV ratings service in that country. A similar situation obtained in European broadcasting in those countries that had commercial television (such as Britain from 1955).

The partnership between the big brands and the new media was seen from the outset as problematic by social activists. In 1957, Vance Packard wrote an indictment of this alliance in his widely read work *The Hidden Persuaders*. A culture in which products are sold as surrogates for human emotional needs is, Packard argued, asking for trouble. Since then, the whole brand image-making enterprise has come constantly under attack from all ideological directions (Key 1972, 1976, 1980). Right-of-centre groups attack the brand-media partnership for promoting secular humanism and promiscuity, and left-wing ones do so for the partnership's deceitfully promoting unabashed consumerism and thus damaging the psychosocial fiber of human society. But, to this day, no real, serious evidence of negative effects from this partnership has come forth. Moreover, it is hard to accept the views of many critics and anti-

Table 2.1 Taxonomy of human needs and motives (based on Straubhaar and LaRose 2000)

Motives	Needs
Achievement	The need to achieve meaningful objectives in life
Affiliation	The need to win acceptance
Consistency	The need to ensure order and routine
Diversion	The need to enjoy oneself
Dominance	The need to exert influence in relations
Independence	The need to be self-reliant
Novelty	The need to have new things
Nurturing	The need to care for others and be cared for by others
Popularity	The need to win the attention of others
Recognition	The need to be recognized
Security	The need to be free from harm and threat
Sexuality	The need to express sexuality
Stimulation	The need to have one's senses stimulated
Support	The need to receive support
Understanding	The need to teach and instruct

consumerist groups for the reason that they themselves seem rather willing to live comfortably within the consumerist lifestyle patterns of the very social system they decry.

However, what is worrisome about our "branded culture" is the fact that it taps into basic psychological needs to ensure that products are bought, whether they are needed or not. As Straubhaar and LaRose (2000: 371) point out, these are built directly into brand imagery. Since brands are signs that stand for ideas with a strong emotional appeal, it is worthwhile reproducing Straubhaar and LaRose's list of needs and motives in Table 2.1.

In effect, the promotion of products in a modern consumerist culture is based on the principle that people will buy things if they perceive them as satisfying some basic emotion, desire, or social need. For example, some brands exploit fear or shame constantly as their basic ploy in promoting their ware. As a case in point, TV commercials on a variety of lifestyle and cosmetic products shown on Italian television were recorded and examined by the Toronto–Lugano research team 2002 (see Acknowledgments). Of the nearly 70 such commercials recorded, 52 were structured around a subtext of fear—fear of marginalization, ostracism, etc. from a peer group. Table 2.2 is a sampling.

Table 2.2 Sampling of Italian television commercials (2002) structured around the subtext of fear

Brand	Product	Fear subtext
Axe	Shower gel	Fear of ostracism because of bad body odor
Dove	Deodorant	Fear of social marginalization
Heineken	Beer	Fear of social marginalization
Impulse	Women's deodorant	Fear of having an unattractive body image
Plasmon	Biscuits	Fear of not providing the best for one's kids
Pop-up	Condoms	Fear of being labeled by peers as reckless
Solero Algida	Sorbet ice-cream	Fear of social marginalization
Tim Daddy	Cell phones	Fear of being left out of peer group
Tissot	Watches	Fear of not being cool

It is estimated that the average citizen living in a consumerist culture is exposed to over 3,000 advertisements a day and watches three years' worth of television commercials over the course of a lifetime (Kilbourne 1999). Everywhere one turns, one is bound to find some message designed to persuade people to buy some product, to endorse a political candidate, to support a cause, etc. Business firms, political candidates, social organizations, special-interest groups, and governments alike advertise routinely to create favorable images of themselves in the minds of people. And these are being constantly updated and renewed, creating a sense that they are evolving along with society generally. Budweiser beer, for instance, is constantly creating new humorous images of its brand which allow it to keep in step with the changing times and with changing trends within its target market—young males. The humor used is consistent with that used on TV sitcoms and in cinema. It is the kind of humor that makes the brand appear contemporary and "relevant"—from Budweiser's "Whassup" campaign in which a social expression taken from hip-hop culture in the early 2000s to the use of sports celebrities such as Tiger Woods by such brands as Nike shoes to create images that have an instant appeal to sports fans and young people generally. As a result, a dynamic interplay between the brand and lifestyle trends has emerged, whereby one influences the other synergistically—the talk and look of actors in popular commercials becomes the talk and look of people in society; and fashions and idiomatic expressions that already exist in society are adopted by advertisers to reinforce certain trends. As Twitchell (2000: 1) aptly puts it, "language about products and services has pretty much replaced language about all other subjects." The "semiosphere," as the Estonian semiotician Yuri Lotman (1922–93) called the culture, has become almost completely branded (Lotman 1991). Brands are no longer perceived to be just "things" for consumption, but mainly as vehicles for securing a better job, protecting oneself against the hazards of old age and illness, attaining popularity and personal prestige, obtaining praise from others, increasing pleasure, advancing socially, and maintaining health.

As Twitchell (2004) has argued, there is little today that has not been branded—i.e. given an identity akin to a brand product. Religions, personalities, and even sports (the UEFA Champions League, NBA brand, the Powergen Challenge Cup, etc.) are now branded. And it is not just a metaphorical use of the word "brand" that is involved, but a veritable process of using the brand product model in other (if not most) domains of culture. There is now a constant dynamic interplay between cultural trends and the promotion of brand products through ad campaigns. The "Whassup" campaign mentioned above is a perfect case in point. Budweiser created scenes of African–American single men, around 30 years of age, each greeting the other with a hip-hop salutation, "Whassup?" As Holt (2004: 177) observes, this was a "passkey into a shared worldview, a complete sign of brotherly solidarity." The phrase "Whassup?" thus became branded (associated with the Budweiser product), although it was originally extracted from an existing, but emotionally meaningful, subculture.

The reason why branding has become such a pervasive force in culture is, arguably, because the naming process is a cultural act. At a practical social level, naming a product, like naming a human being, has an identification function—i.e. it allows consumers literally to name which product they desire to purchase (or not). At another level, however, it brings the product into the realm of cultural signification, where it links up with a constellation of culture-specific meanings that are associated with the product. Consider a pair of shoes named after a "high-class" manufacturer such as Gucci. At a literal level, the Gucci name allows us to identify the actual type of shoe we may desire to buy. But this is not all it does—it also assigns an aura of artistry, craftsmanship, fashionability, and superior quality to the product. The shoes are perceived to be the "work" of an Italian shoe artist—Gucci—not just an assembly-line product for common folk to wear. This added meaning is the brand image that the product name is designed to evoke in people. By psychological extension, therefore, the perception crystallizes that buying Gucci shoes is buying a work of shoe art. This is an unconscious process. In the fashion industry, designer brands such as Gucci, Armani, and Calvin Klein evoke similar images. They are felt to be objets d'art, rather than mere clothing or cosmetic items; so too do names such as Ferrari, Lamborghini, and Maserati in the domain of automobiles. The manufacturer's name, in such cases, extends the social and psychological meanings of the product considerably, by associating it with the traditions of artistic authorship. The artist is someone who is perceived to create works of aesthetic value. An Armani suit is thus not perceived to be merely "something to wear." It is something created by a clothing artist. The Armani brand can thus be said to summon forth a "signification system" for the product that has nothing to do with the literal functions of clothing.

In a phrase, buying an Armani or a Gucci product provides the impression of buying a work of fashion art to be displayed on the body. Studying the nature of this kind of cultural extension of meaning is the sum and substance of cultural semiotics, as will be discussed shortly. Like every name, a brand is a sign. As such, it has both an identification function, known as its "denotative" function, and a cultural function, known as its "connotative" function. The latter generally evokes unconscious associations of meaning that are built into the name itself. Buying a perfume named Poison (by Christian Dior), for instance, imparts the implicit feeling of buying a dangerous, but alluring, love potion; buying Moondrops, Natural Wonder, Rainflower, Sunsilk, and Skin Dew cosmetic items conveys the feeling that one is acquiring some of nature's beauty resources; buying Eterna 27, Clinique, Endocil, or Equalia beauty products conveys a vague sense that one is getting scientifically tested products, etc. Unnamed products do not engender such arrays of implicit meanings.

The phenomenon of name-giving in the human species is a fascinating one on many counts. In a sense, each person is a brand—an individual with an identity that is largely a construction derived from specific cultural traditions. Across cultures, newborn children are not considered full-fledged members of their society until they are given an appropriate name tying them to it. The act of naming infants is the first symbolic rite of passage in a society—a rite that has the function of assigning to them a unique personality—a brand identity, if you will. If the family does not give the infant a name, then society will step in to do so. From childhood onward, the individual's sense of self is felt somehow to be mirrored in his or her name. In Inuit cultures, an individual is perceived to have a body, a soul, and a name; a person is not seen as complete without all three. The Inuit also believe that a newborn baby cries because it wants its name, and will not be fulfilled spiritually until it gets it. Names are commonly believed across the world to have the power to foretell a person's destiny, or else to pass on to infants the spiritual qualities of the individuals who have previously shared the name. In many Native American cultures, for instance, an ancestral name is thought to cast a magical, protective spell on the child given the name. This is why many indigenous people will refuse to say their name out loud, fearing that this "senseless" act could break the magical spell. But even in Western culture, we give our children the names of ancestors with the implicit belief that the character or the protection of the ancestor might be passed on to the newborn. In 1968, a British television series called *The Prisoner*, which subsequently became a classic, featured as one of its themes the perception that one's sense of self is wrapped up in one's given name. It portrayed a captive community of ex-government officers who were assigned numbers instead of traditional names—*Number 1*, *Number 2*, etc. The specific idea here was, obviously, that people could be made to conform to the will of the state if they did not have a name. The use of numerical identification of prisoners and slaves is, in effect, a negation of their humanity and, ultimately, their existence.

BRANDS AS MENTAL CONSTRUCTS

As Bedbury has perceptively remarked: "Every brand has a fundamental essence that is not physical or defined exclusively or entirely by products or services" (2002: 12). It is thus both a physical object and a mental object. In human life, there is virtually no object or artifact that is not imbued with meaning. Brands are, in effect, "mental constructs," or "fundamental essences," as Bedbury characterizes them, that evoke a broad range of meanings. The jewelry, clothes, furniture, ornaments, tools, toys, etc. that the marketplace makes available would be perceived as "senseless objects" without branding. Branding links them to cultural traditions, values, rituals, etc. They thus provide valuable clues as to what meanings are important to a culture.

In a phrase, the "essences" that constitute brands are powerful because they have social and cultural relevance. Take beer as an example. Beer is beer, with varying degrees of flavor and strength to it. But beer has social relevance built into it. It is a drink that is commonly used in specific social situations (and not others), especially among friends and peers (but rarely at formal celebratory events), and thus has social symbolism built into it—a fact that is exploited by advertising campaigns by brand beers such as Budweiser and Corona. What kinds of people drink Budweiser or Corona beer? Answers to this question would typically include remarks about the educational level, class, social attitudes, worldview, etc. of the consumer. The one who drinks Budweiser is perceived by people as vastly different from the one who drinks Corona. The former is portrayed in advertising campaigns as a youngish down-to-earth male who simply wants to "hang out with the guys"; the latter as a more sophisticated type (male or female) who appreciates the finer things of life. The two beer brands speak directly to different *types* of individuals, so that they can see their own personalities mirrored in the lifestyle images created by advertising campaigns, and thus identify with one or the other beer brand.

Branding adds a dimension to products that was absent from the marketplaces of the past—"cultural meaning" which in semiotics is known more specifically as "connotative meaning." And the more of such meaning that can be built into a brand, the more likely it will become itself socialized (spread into the social mindset). The cultural meanings of brands can hardly be pinned down exactly. They can only be inferred. They are, in a phrase, "mental constructs." These can be defined simply as the culturally shaped images that come to mind in relation to a specific brand. Take, as a case in point, the Amazon.com name—originally a Web-based bookstore with a database of millions of titles. The Amazon part of the name suggests at least two connotative meaning levels. At one level, it reverberates with mythic overtones. In Greek mythology, the Amazons were a race of warlike women who excluded men from their society. The suggestion of a bold new world of strong women who possess secret knowledge and abilities is not a casual one. There are few people who will perceive in that name anything to the contrary. This is why speakers of English use it metaphorically to describe females who are tall and gigantic (e.g. "She's an Amazon"). At another connotative level, the Amazon name evokes an image of one of the earth's largest natural and still largely unexplored areas, the Brazilian Amazon region, thus challenging computer users to enter by analogy into its own unexplored world and navigate it.

The mental construction process is a largely unconscious one. We do not see in our mind the Amazon jungle or gigantic women controlling a certain domain of cyberspace. We get, instead, a vague, nebulous feeling of the power of the website to get us what we want. We can, of course, bring the "Amazon imagery" to consciousness by reflecting upon it. But such reflection is rare in the routine everyday use of signs. Brand names suggest images; but these are never specific or clear-cut. They are understandable only within larger associations of cultural meaning.

Consider, as further examples, the Revlon, Captain Morgan, and Pepsi brand products. Revlon was founded in 1932 by Charles Revson, with his brother Joseph and chemist Charles Lachman. The brand name is a slight modification of Revson's name. Revlon lipstick and nail enamel became an instant market success story among female consumers, possibly because it was promoted with exotic names such as Tropic Sky, rather than merely descriptive ones such dark red, medium red, pink, etc. The images that the Revlon names evoke are abstract ones associated with the exotic world of nature. The Captain Morgan rum brand, on the one hand, is an example of a product eliciting a fictitious image. Although no such personage has ever existed, one can easily imagine a rum-drinking pirate with the name of "Captain Morgan." Such images are those that reproduce some sensory quality or property in the mind. The Pepsi brand name, on the other hand, has an auditory sensory quality to it that is imitative of the sound made by the soft drink as it fizzes in a drinking glass or the reaction we get by putting our face near the fizz.

The type of image evoked by Amazon.com also requires further commentary, given that it is an image rooted in a mythic tradition, rendering it psychologically powerful. The process by which such imagery is evoked can be called, simply, "mythologization." Mythologization is a common feature in the advertising of lifestyle products. As a concrete example, consider a 2004 ad used by Gucci to promote a purse product. In it, one is first struck by rather powerful visual signifiers—black snakes completely surrounding a delicate, small purse, almost strangling it. Clearly, these suggest a chain of mythic meanings that are associated with black snakes, including fear, darkness, and evil. Since ancient times, snakes have been feared in many cultures because of their deadly venom. They have been used as symbols with this meaning in narratives of all kinds. They also evoke phallic symbolism in the traditions of many cultures. These two chains of meaning seem to be built into the visual imagery of the ad, which shows slithering snakes in an embrace, thus suggesting phallic copulation, since snakes only come into close proximity when they form "mating balls" in which they frantically try to mate with a single female.

The chainlike handle of the purse and the metal handcuff-like clasp in the center add yet another mythic element to the "implicit sexuality" of the scene, given that chains and handcuffs evoke images of sexual bondage. Conversely, the chain and handcuffs may also suggest an image of the female protecting herself from the slithery males. Other Gucci ads of the period (2004–5) were based on similar imagery. Mythic constructs of this type are powerful because they bestow upon a brand the timelessness and universality that we associate with primordial mythic narration.

At this stage, a few words about myth and mythologization are needed. Both terms draw from the work of the French semiotician Roland Barthes (1915–80). Famously, in *Mythologies* (1957; English translation 1973), Barthes drew together a series of brief articles he had written for magazines in the period 1954–6 to demonstrate different aspects of the myth of French life and society. Central to his formulation of myth was the tracking down in the "decorative display of *what-goes-without-saying*, the ideological abuse which, in my view, is hidden" (1973: 11). For Barthes, it is not just heroic stories that qualify for mythic status; *anything* is susceptible to myth, especially the most everyday of phenomena. As he argues, "nothing can be safe from myth" (1973: 131). For Barthes, myth is the domain of stereotypes and other means of fixing limits to representation.

Most importantly, though, is the way that myth is "spoken." As we have seen, objects of everyday life take on "second-order" or "connotative" meanings. As such, the semiotic act that such objects must embody comprises a process of denotation (straightforward indicating) and connotation (associations). Yet what Barthes makes clear in *Mythologies* is that connotation, even though it is "second-order," generally happens first in signs—i.e. connotations or associations are so strong because they draw on the massive power of the social and ideological worlds. What denotation does is to "naturalize" them into a myth. Those connotations that border on the outrageous or unbelievable are rendered credible by virtue of being part of a system of denotation—such as the starkly realistic photography in the Gucci ad. So when we proceed by assuming that brands have second meanings tagged on to them—as is inevitable in the kinds of analyses carried out in this book which uncover semiotic strategies—we should remember this point. The act of mythologization is a harnessing of ideas with strong emotional appeal in a sign (or sign system) which makes the representation credible or a seemingly normal part of everyday life.

Mythologization is also commonly built into logo design, as will be discussed further in subsequent chapters. The logo is the nonverbal counterpart of the brand name. Take as an example the McDonald's golden arches logo. The arches reverberate with mythic symbolism, beckoning good people to march through them triumphantly into a paradise of order, cleanliness, friendliness, hospitality, hard work, self-discipline, family values. From the menu to the uniforms, McDonald's exacts and imposes standardization. McDonald's is a place that will "do it all for you," as one of the company's slogans of the past so aptly phrased it. All we have to do is go through the arches.

As the foregoing discussion has intended to argue, the difference between a brand and a product is a strategic one that has rather profound psychological implications. A product has no identity; a brand does. It garners an identity through its name, its association with cultural meaning, its dissemination through mass manufacturing and advertising campaigns, and other strategies designed to give it what can be called "cultural relevance." Brands now offer the same kinds of promises and hopes to which religions once held exclusive rights—security against the hazards of old age, better positions in life, popularity and personal prestige, social advancement, better health, happiness, etc. In a phrase, the modern brand manufacturer stresses not the product, but the benefits that may be expected to ensue from its purchase. And, as we shall see throughout this book, the image-maker is becoming more and more adept at setting foot into the same subconscious regions of psychic experience that were once explored only by philosophers, artists, and religious thinkers.

SIGNIFICATION SYSTEMS

As mentioned above, a brand is a *sign* in the semiotic sense. It stands for something other than itself in some meaningful or meaning-bearing way. Equivalent words used for "brand" in other languages bring this out concretely. In Italian, for instance, it is *marca* or *marchio*, "mark," which is in actual fact the definition of the Greek word *semeion*. The semiotic study of brands is, fundamentally, a study of a particular kind of "semeion."

As we have seen, Barthes was one of the first to emphasize the need to study signs of this kind with the tools of semiotics. Barthes had argued in *Mythologies* that contemporary consumerist lifestyles promoted an unhealthy craving for new goods. He called this culture-generated syndrome "neomania," which he defined as an obsessive desire for new objects of consumption. Modern consumerist cultures, he claimed, elevated shopping to much more than acquiring the essentials required for daily living; they bestowed upon it the same kinds of meanings that we associate with myth and ritual.

The logic of Barthes's perspective can be seen in the kinds of advertising campaigns that involve mythologization. Take, as one particular example, the advertising campaign used by Absolut Vodka in the mid-1990s which played on religious themes: in one particular ad, the image of a halo around the vodka bottle can be seen with the caption "Absolut Perfection"; in another, a bottle with wings and the caption "Absolut Heaven" was shown; and in yet another, a bottle held by the hand of a medieval knight with the caption "Absolut Grail" was exposed (in medieval legend the grail was the plate or cup from which Christ drank at the Last Supper and which Joseph of Arimathea used to receive the blood from the wounds of the crucified Christ). The overall message of the campaign was rather transparent—spirituality could be obtained by imbibing the vodka. The ads effectively brought out the meaning of the brand name itself—the "absolute" is often perceived as designating the "afterlife" and "truth."

Incidentally, Absolut Vodka's advertising strategy has always been to equate the drink with myth and art. Its website has always contained numerous works of modern art commissioned especially for it. In the late 1990s, it showed Absolut Panushka, a set of short films by 24 contemporary experimental animators, plus introductory pages by another 12 artists, all arranged by animator Christine Panushka. Those works ran the gamut from images hand-painted directly onto film to high-tech computer animation by artists from around the world.

After the publication of *Mythologies*, semiotic theory became widely used within the fields of *critical analysis*, a branch of cultural studies that examines the relationship between people and media genres, advertising, consumer products, etc., and *functional analysis*, a branch of sociology that studies media institutions and their effects on individual and group behavior. Scholars from both these fields were attracted particularly to Barthes's notion that the meaning structures built into consumerist symbols and pop-culture spectacles were related to those that characterized the ancient myths.

In the 1960s, another French semiotician, Jean Baudrillard (1929–), continued where Barthes left off. Like his compatriot, Baudrillard scathingly attacked the consumerist world as one large distraction-producing enterprise creating images of material objects for no other purpose than to get people to purchase them (e.g. Baudrillard 1973, 1978, 1981, 1988). However, the critiques of Barthes and Baudrillard, as well-meaning as they were, may have unintentionally "overpoliticized" semiotics. Nevertheless, the interest in semiotics on the part of the business community itself in the last few years has been remarkable—confirming in large part the notion that branding is a semiotic act. From websites that overtly embrace semiotics as the basis for giving advice to clients to sites that refer to the discipline in some way, there seems to be a growing awareness in the business world that the only truly insightful approach to branding is to study how brands create arrays of meanings.

To the semiotician, meanings do not exist in any absolute sense, but in relation to other meanings. They cohere, in other words, into "systems" often called "codes," that can be defined simply as organizational meaning grids that keep signs distinct by a series of relations among them. As a simple example, consider the alphabet letter "A." At a denotative level, it is a sign whose function and meaning can only be determined with respect to the other signs in the system known as the English alphabet—a letter standing for a mid-vowel sound. It has signifying "value," as Saussure (1916: 45) called it, because it can be compared, contrasted, and related to the other letter signs in the system. In terms of the alphabet sequence, it can also be defined as the "first" letter. Now, if we look at the uses of "A" outside the alphabet code, it becomes obvious that it is involved in a host of other meaning-making activities, related to the fact that it is the "first letter"—e.g. it is used in Western schools and universities as the "top grade" assigned to student achievement; it is found commonly in descriptions of products such as "A-grade" types of oil; it is used as a variable in algebra, etc. In these and other uses, the "A" cuts across codes of various kinds. In each case, however, the initial "meaning imprint" of "first among letters" is implicit, overtly or implicitly. As mentioned above, these are the connotative meanings of this particular sign. Each sign in the alphabet "code" acquires signifying value (denotative and connotative) in similar ways.

As is well known, modern-day semiotic method is based on the writings of the American logician Charles S. Peirce (1839–1914) and the French philologist Ferdinand de Saussure (1857–1913). But the origin of this science can be traced to the ancient world. The term "semiotics" was used by the founder of Western medical science, Hippocrates (460–377 BCE), to indicate the study of symptoms, since these were signs that stood for physical conditions and ailments of various kinds. Discovering what they stand for, Hippocrates claimed, is the crux of medical diagnosis. As a diagnostic science, semiotics was further developed by Galen (AD 129–c. 199), perhaps the most outstanding physician of antiquity after Hippocrates. Galen saw symptoms as forms with recurring and thus predictable physical characteristics, allowing the practitioner to decipher the connection between the forms and the conditions they suggested.

Semiotic analysis generally consists of the exact same procedure— relating the physical form of signs to what they stand for. Take the example of the alphabet character "X." This has a noticeable physical appearance that can be described in concrete terms—a letter of the alphabet constructed by two intersecting lines. This physical part of the sign is sometimes called the "signifier" by some semioticians (although its relation to Saussure's idea of a signifier is tenuous) and "representamen" by Peirce. Now, at a literal level, this signifier refers to the twenty-fourth letter of the English alphabet. This is what some semioticians call the

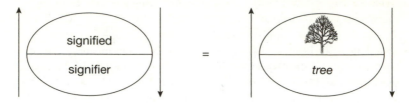

Figure 2.1 Saussure's model of the sign

"signified" (although not Saussure's signified, which was a "mental concept") and Peirce the *object*. But the "diagnosis" of X does not stop there. In mathematics, for example, it is used as the symbol for an unknown quantity or variable and thus, by extension, an unknown or unnamed factor, thing, or person. It is also used as a signature by anyone who is unable to write one's name. It is also a sign designating a sexually explicit movie. All these meanings constitute meanings that reach out beyond the denotative and, as we have seen, Barthes called such meanings "second-order" and the whole process of connotative extension "signification." Peirce used the term "interpretant" instead to indicate that all constellations of meanings are ultimately interpretations of some type or other—personal, social, historical, etc.

Perhaps the most important aspect to note about the sign is that the connection between the sign as physical form and its meaning, once established, is bidirectional—one implies the other. As Saussure observed, when we use the word "tree," which produces an acoustic image in the brain, the visual image of the plant comes instantly to mind (Figure 2.1).

The foregoing discussion is a highly simplified one, doing short shrift to the richness of sign theory, whether it be Saussurean or Peircean. However, the objective of this book is not to enter into the nature of semiotic modeling, nor does it intend to compare the two models (Saussurean and Peircean), but rather simply to adopt the "diagnostic" approach of semiotics—medical or cultural—that sees signs as standing for meanings, conditions, ideas, etc. by virtue of the relations they have with other signs. Take, for example, the Triple XXX brand name given to a Canadian beer. The association with something "forbidden but desirable," such as an XXX-rated movie, is transparently obvious to those who know the semiotic code—the relations that X has to other domains of cultural meaning. In cultures where erotic movies do not exist (and may be unknown), it constitutes a signifier with no meaning—it is what Barthes called an "empty signifier." However, in Western culture,

Table 2.3 Examples of signification systems built into certain brands

Brand	Images it evokes	Signification system (interpretive key)
Camels cigarettes	"Cigarettes smoked in fashionable clubs"	The camel suggests desert adventure, which has always had a romantic allure in narrative portrayals, as portrayed, for example, in the 1942 movie Casablanca
Gucci shoes	"High fashion," "artistic," etc.	Because the brand is "signed" by the maker it is perceived as having been made by an artist; it constitutes a work of "shoe art"
Macintosh computers	"User-friendly," "highly functional," and "attractive computer (preferred by artists, designers, etc.)"	The "Apple" name and logo suggest the biblical theme of "forbidden knowledge" and "temptation," and along with it the Eve story
Marlboro cigarettes	"Cigarettes smoked by rugged, male individuals," "the American loner"	Smoking the cigarette suggests a cowboy-type machismo that was once a staple of Hollywood movies

it summons forth images of such movies. In this way, the name Triple XXX evokes an unconscious array of connotations associated with such movies. By the way, it can also mean "extra strong," thus expanding the connotative range of the brand. This "double-meaning" value has been applied to the name of a Hollywood personage—agent "Triple XXX." It alludes not only to the activities that the character can perform physically, which are "forbidden" to the rest of humankind, but also to his super-human strength.

In effect, the meanings evoked by the Triple XXX brand form a signification system—a constellation of (connotative) meanings suggested by its name. The interpretive key to deciphering brand image is, in my view, the signification system (or code) itself. To avoid the non-semiotic meanings that the term "code" entails in English—a collection of laws, a systematic collection of rules (e.g. the traffic code), etc.—I will use that term "signification system" from now on. Table 2.3 gives some examples of signification systems built into common brands.

A signification system can be defined, simply, as the set of culture-specific meanings and attendant mental constructs that are evoked by a brand. These systems are established because a brand, being a sign, enters into relations with other signs in a culture gaining its "value" from them. These systems are created initially either by the brand name (or logo) itself or by the cultural symbolism its name evokes—as such they are produced by iconic, symbolic, or indexical brand names.

As two concrete examples of iconically generated signification systems, take the Acura brand of Japanese automobiles and the Yahoo search engine. The obvious suggestion of "accuracy" in automobile design and performance is evoked by the physical constitution of the name itself, which not only imitates the English word "accuracy," but also Japanese word structure—e.g. tempura. The brand name thus reinforces, by itself, its connection to Japanese culture and, thus, to the widely held view that Japan is at the cutting edge of technology. But, in addition, the signifier suggests the phonetic structure of Italian words. The "a" ending of the name indicates the feminine gender in Italian grammar and thus, by metaphorical extension, the allure of feminine beauty. These implicit meanings constitute the signification system built into the name Acura. In the case of brand-naming practices, however, onomatopoeia and other kinds of simulative strategies are more the rule than the exception. Similarly, the name Yahoo suggests, at one level, an expression of joy and spontaneous excitement. The word was coined by Jonathan Swift (1667–1745) in his novel *Gulliver's Travels* (1726) to refer to a member of a race of brutes having human form. By its very sound, it continues to evoke images of "brute excitement."

The names Acura and Yahoo are examples of what Peirce called "iconic" signs— i.e. signs that simulate some property of their referents. Iconic brand names tend to be more easily remembered—e.g. Splash (detergent) evokes through sound imitation what is done with the product ("splashing"); the "Polo" logo, which represents the sport of polo visually with a horse and a rider dressed in polo garb), etc.

As examples of symbolically based signification system consider, again, the Apple brand of computer along with the Jeep and Saturn motor vehicles. The purpose of computers is, denotatively, to help us carry out certain tasks (such as word processing) efficiently, accurately, and quickly. But the brand name, logo, and product design of Apple Mac computers does much more, since they reach into the realm of cultural symbolism. The brand thus generates a symbolic signification system that can be characterized as an "Eve code," whereby the apple stands for forbidden knowledge from which the mother of humanity took a fateful bite. Mac computers are, in fact, not only user-friendly, but can also be said to be suggestive of feminine beauty. Although this is somewhat reductive, there is little doubt that an Eve code is, at the very least, a latent factor in how we perceive the Apple brand of computer.

The Jeep vehicle is a durable, general-purpose motor vehicle with four-wheel drive and a quarter-ton capacity; the Saturn is a smaller automobile that is recognizable by the "curvy shape" of its frame. The Jeep was first mass-produced for the US armed forces in 1940. Combining the ruggedness of a truck with the mobility of a car, the original Jeep carried six passengers and traveled about 105 km/h (about 65 mph). Its powerful engine, two- and four-wheel drive, and deep-treaded tires allow for easy maneuverability over difficult terrain. All these structural features of its design are consistent with the "military code" that constitutes the signification system. The Saturn automobile, on the other hand, evokes a different kind of system. In Roman mythology, Saturn was the god of agriculture. In later legends he was identified with the Greek god Cronus, who ruled during the Golden Age, a time of perfect peace and happiness. The Saturn brand produces a signification system that is based on this mythical "Saturn code," and this would explain why the Saturn Company is perceived as "customer-friendly" and sensitive to nature (being designed as a highly "environmentally friendly" vehicle).

Indexically produced signification systems are those that are evoked by brand names that constitute information on what a product can do— e.g. Easy Off, Handy Wipes, Renuzit (= "Renews it"). An *index* is a sign that serves to guide, point out, or otherwise facilitate reference.

It should be mentioned, at this point, that there is another meaning to the term "iconicity" that must be mentioned here—given that business people often talk about "iconic brands"—namely, the obvious relation that the term "icon" has to the religious icon, whose mystical and narrative imagery imbues it with a powerful emotional quality. The word "icon" goes back, in fact, to the Byzantine empire of the first centuries CE, when the emperor dispatched portraits of himself to the farthest corners of the empire to ensure that he would not be forgotten. The portraits depicted not only his likeness, but also his power, despite his absence, and thus symbolized the unity of the empire under his rule. The early Christians adopted the icon tradition and applied it to the domain of sacredness, investing their images with a mystical interpretation so as to convey the message of the new religion to the illiterate masses.

Icons have thus always held a deeper symbolic meaning. In line with the Platonic tradition of the era, the icon and the idea were thought to be one and the same. They were perceived as mirrors of ideas and truths. The original icons came to represent the indivisibility of church and state, especially since the emperor occupied a special position as an intermediary between the faithful, the priest, and God. Icons were put in churches everywhere and sold to the faithful in the medieval period. In a sense, every brand is an icon. As with religious icons, people like brand-named products, want to have them, and read many meanings into them. They are also elements of recruitment and communication, based on a corporate identity (religious or commercial), in the form of a transmittable, consistent identity.

It can also be argued that the brand is a "fetish." Fetishism is the conviction that some objects, known as "fetishes" (from Portuguese *feitiço*, "artificial, charm," from Latin *facticius* "artificial"), are imbued with supernatural attributes. The fetish is typically a figure modeled or carved from clay, stone, wood, or some other material, resembling a deified animal or some sacred object. Sometimes it is the animal itself, or a tree, river, rock, or place associated with it. In some societies, belief in the powers of the fetish is so strong that fetishism develops into idolatry. In such cases, the belief system is referred to as an extreme form of animism—the view that spirits either inhabit or communicate with humans through material objects. The term "fetishism" has been applied in our culture to describe sexual urges and fantasies that persistently involve the use of objects by themselves or, at times, with a sexual partner. Common fetishes in our society are feet, shoes, and articles of intimate female apparel.

Fetishism is not limited to tribal or pre-modern cultures. On the contrary, it is alive and well in modern cultures, in the form of products. In the 1970s, for example, American society went mad for "pet rocks." Many considered the fad a ploy foisted on a gullible public spoiled by consumerism by a crafty manufacturer, and thus simply a quick way to make money. But to a semiotician, that craze could not have been perpetrated in the first place, unless some signifying force was at work—and that force was fetishism.

There are several caveats that must be stated clearly when dealing with the semiotic study of brands. First, the degree to which the signification systems generated by certain brands will induce consumers to buy products is an open question. In any case, it is certainly not the point of semiotic analysis to determine this, although it would seem logical to assume that any branding strategy that is effective *semiotically* is probably also going to be effective *psychologically*. Needless to say, if the results of semiotic analysis expose the "hidden meaning structures" that can be deemed to be counterproductive to a culture's psychological well-being, then so be it (for a review of the relevant semiotic research, see Mick, Burroughs, Hetzel, and Brannen 2004). In fact, the outcome of semiotic analysis, like that of physics, can be an incentive for social activism.

Physicists provide atomic theories, not the means of making atomic power stations; semioticians provide theories of meaning, not the means of using meaning systems for profit.

It is relevant to note that brand-naming and advertising are among the most strictly regulated enterprises in North America (and in other parts of the world). This is a consequence of the "awareness-raising" that the many critical social scientific studies on branding and advertising have brought about in recent years. But legislation is hardly the most effective way of protecting people against the brand's persuasive power. Real "immunization" comes from the signification systems that are triggered by brands, not in regulating or censoring advertising.

Branding products is, ultimately, a social act. It "reifies" the product, service, or company inserting it as an element in the web of meanings that constitute a culture—"reification" is the term used in philosophy referring to the actualizing of something that is conceptual in real ways. It is equivalent to the process of bringing human beings into the social order by giving them a name. That act reifies human beings as individuals, transforming them into "persons." Brands have, in effect, been anthropomorphically transformed into personalities with identities that have become merged with those of consumers. One feeds off the other.

As we will see in Chapter 3, brand naming is an important strategy of brand management but it requires other strategies, too: slogans/ jingles, package and product design, and the perennial work of advertising.

3

BRAND IMAGE

In real life, unlike in Shakespeare, the sweetness of the rose depends upon the name it bears. Things are not only what they are. They are, in very important respects, what they seem to be.

Hubert H. Humphrey (1911–78)

In Aeschylus' (525–456 BCE) drama *Prometheus Bound*, the hero Prometheus, tied to a rock, proclaimed prophetically that one day "rulers would conquer and control not by strength, nor by violence, but by cunning." In Greek mythology, Prometheus was the friend and benefactor of humanity. He and his brother Epimetheus were given the task of creating humans and animals, and then providing them with the endowments they would need to survive. After Prometheus went to heaven and stole fire from the gods to give to humanity, he incurred the wrath of Zeus, who had him chained to a rock. There, he was constantly preyed upon by an eagle until Hercules freed him. The statement that Prometheus uttered as he was tied to the rock contains a warning that is as insightful today as it was at the dawn of civilization.

The strategies that the brand "rulers" use are indeed "cunning" ones. Like Prometheus, they promise to provide humanity with the endowments it will need to survive, whether it is a McDonald's hamburger, Cheerios cereal, Nike shoes, or Armani suits. Like Prometheus, brands now make "humans" and "animals," naming them Mr Clean, Tony the Tiger, etc. The brand congeners seem indeed to want to "conquer and control by cunning," as Prometheus warned.

Figure 3.1 State Farm Insurance Companies® (with kind permission)

The purpose of this chapter is to take an initial look at some of the strategies used by the Prometheans of the brand world. There are five main ones: (1) devising an appropriate name for the product, service, or corporation, which, as discussed in the previous chapter, is a critical strategy; (2) designing a suitable logo for it; (3) inventing some slogan or jingle that explicates, illustrates, and reinforces the brand's image; (4) designing the product or its container in a related way (wherever applicable); and (5) preparing advertising texts that put the brand's signification system on display in various ways. As a preliminary example of this, consider the State Farm company. Its name (State Farm) evokes "down-on-the-farm" values, especially friendliness and trustworthiness. Its logo communicates the same kind of image or signification system—three touching circles encased in a square with round vertices—given that circles stand for groups of people sharing an interest, activity, or achievement (Figure 3.1).

It uses a slogan/jingle ("Like a good neighbor, State Farm is there") that enunciates and reinforces the same signification system. It also creates ads and commercials that portray State Farm employees as wholesome, neighborly individuals ready to help out in time of need. The State Farm brand promises that the insurance company will "live up to its name."

THE CONNOTATIVE INDEX

The State Farm signification system is commonly referred to as "brand image" in the relevant marketing literature. To the semiotician, this term needs further refinement, since the "image" in it refers not to the denotative value of the brand, but to its connotative one. As mentioned in the previous chapter, signs possess two levels of meaning in tandem. The denotative level is the constant (or basic) meaning that a sign bears. This allows us basically to identify the product (or service) a brand stands for. Note that denotation implies that the referent (product) is a generic one, not a specific one. For example, it is irrelevant whether the Gucci brand of shoes is for women or men, whether they are a size 9 or 10, or whether they are brown or black, etc.—as long as the shoe is a Gucci shoe. At a different, and emotionally more powerful level, the Gucci shoe evokes an array of different, culturally relevant meanings. As mentioned in the previous chapter, these are the connotations that the brand evokes. Shoes are protective gear. However, at the connotative level, the Gucci brand is linked to the culturally shaped symbolism of elegance and artistry.

The higher the number of connotations a brand generates, the greater its psychological force. The greater the number, the greater its "connotative index" (CI), as it may be called. This is not a mathematical concept; rather, it refers to the relative number of connotations—high, average, low—that a brand tends to produce. These can be measured in a relative way simply by asking subjects what a certain brand (or ad) means. Counting the different interpretations is tantamount to counting the number of different connotations built into it. This is what Beasley *et al.* (2000) did in deriving and testing the viability of the concept of CI. The researchers showed 10 subjects 30 ads and asked them to identify which of the ads they thought produced the most thoughts and meanings in their minds. The authors of the study had themselves rated 10 beforehand as having a *high* CI, 10 as having an *average* CI, and 10 as having a *low* CI. The 10 with the pre-rated high CI (mainly perfume/cologne ads) were, in fact, identified by all the subjects as being highly suggestive and appealing. On average, these produced 12–20 different interpretations. The subjects rated the remaining 20 ads as less suggestive, of which they considered 8 to be relatively more suggestive. These were ads for home products and services (insurance, detergents, etc.) that were also rated beforehand as having average CIs. The remaining 12 were identified as being the least suggestive by the subjects. Of these, only 2 were rated beforehand as having average CIs; the others were pre-rated as having *low* CIs. They were all taken from trade magazines announcing products and services in a straightforward "classified ad" manner, although pictures and various symbols were nevertheless used. The CI can thus be conceived to be a continuum, with zero connotation (pure denotative or informational content) at one end and a maximum connotation point (open-ended, ambivalent, ambiguous content) at the other. Classified ads, ads in trade manuals, and the like tend to fall in the sector of the continuum nearest to the zero end-point, whereas life-style ads tend to fall in the sector that becomes progressively more connotative—the one point.

Subsequent research on the validity of the CI conducted by the Toronto–Lugano research team has corroborated the general findings. One of the most interesting byproducts of the research is that the highest CIs are produced by brands that utilize symbolic signification systems. Mythical symbolism in particular tends to produce very high CIs. Thus, the picture of a perfume bottle in an ad tells us, at a denotative level, that it contains a fragrance of a specific type. But this is really a "semi-otic trigger" for a higher-level signification system that is imbued with layers of symbolic meanings—i.e. although we perceive the bottle at a surface level as a perfume container, at a connotative level its shape, its name, etc. activates our knowledge of the culture-specific connotations that these features evoke.

The foregoing discussion is, in effect, a version of Barthes's (1957) idea of second-order meaning. At a denotative level a word such as "lion" is a signifier with a literal signified—"a large wild member of the cat family that lives in Africa and India." But this itself becomes a signifier that juxtaposes the sign to a connotative level where a second-order signified is evoked—e.g. "somebody very brave, strong, or fierce" (Figure 3.2).

The larger the level of the "connotative signified" above—in terms of numbers of meanings—the greater the CI. As a simple example of how this model presents a simple way of understanding signification systems, consider again the Gucci brand of shoe. Simplifying the discus-sion somewhat for the sake of illustration, we can now say that, denotatively, the name is a signifier that stands for a "shoe made by a company named Gucci" (identifier function), becomes itself a signifier that takes on a second-order connotative signified ("artistry," "elegance," "sexiness," etc.) (Figure 3.3). This is the brand's signification system.

BRAND-NAMING STRATEGIES

The concept of CI can be used as well to evaluate the psychological power of brand names. As mentioned in the previous chapter, it was late in the nineteenth century that American firms began en masse to market packaged goods under brand names. The assignment of a name is the first step in creating brand identity and in establishing a CI for a brand.

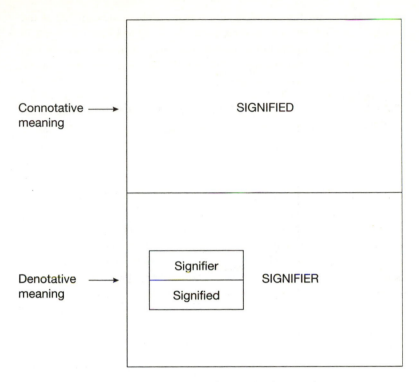

Figure 3.2 A version of Barthes's idea of second-order meaning

Sometimes, the name can consist of simple alphabet characters. One character that seems to have gained favor among brand manufacturers is "X," a letter that appears constantly as well in many areas of pop culture. Research projects undertaken by the present author in early 2005 have revealed that brand names that incorporate X tend to have a higher CI than those that do not. In one early 2005 project, ten subjects were asked to evaluate the brand name Exxon (formerly Esso), by reflecting on the kinds of images that the name itself, and not the product (petroleum oil), evoked. Twenty-nine qualitatively distinct images (second-order meanings) were recorded. Some subjects referred to the two XXs in the name—"It's an exciting name"; "It is a name that is quite sexy-sounding," etc. Others referred to the overall effect that the sound made on them— "tough-sounding," "sounds like it will last"; etc. Others still referred to the overall impressions the word made on them, impressions that included "adventure," "excitement," "daring," etc. A second group of ten

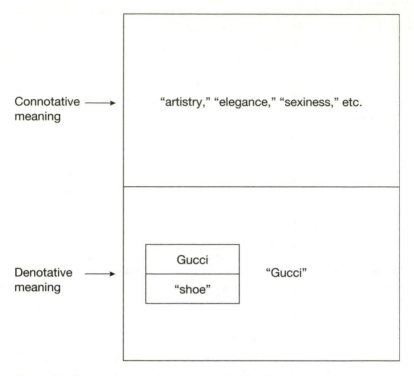

Figure 3.3 Connotative meaning generated by Gucci shoes

subjects was asked instead to evaluate the previous brand name Esso in the same way. In this case, four qualitatively distinct images were recorded that included in different versions the meanings of "softness," "smoothness," "sureness," and "steadiness." Clearly, the Exxon name has a higher CI than does the Esso name, and the probable reason for this is its spelling (with two XXs).

If it were, in fact, demonstrable with further research that X has a high CI, then it would explain the popularity of the twenty-fourth letter of the English alphabet in both branding and pop culture. There's Nissan's X-Terra and X-Trail car models, X-treme sports, the Hollywood action hero Triple X, XXX movies, names of celebrities such as the rapper Xzibit, etc. The letter X is associated with youth, danger, and all the "X-citing" things (pun intended) that commercialist culture makes available. It is interesting to note in this regard that an internet company called X10 used online pop-up ads in 2003 by changing an image and adding a couple of words in order to promote its Xcam2 video camera in 2001. It also included a bedroom on the list of places where the camera could be used. As Reichert (2003: 353) observes: "When coupled with a newly added image of an attractive blonde in revealing clothing, the camera and its potential functions had a whole new set of meanings."

In actual fact, X has been around for centuries as the mathematical variable par excellence, as an ersatz signature used by those who cannot write, as a blasphemous letter assigned to cartoons, as a sign of danger on bottles of alcohol and boxes of dynamite, and as a symbol marking a secret treasure on a pirate's map (Roy 2000). It has thus always connoted danger, mystery, the unexplained, and other occult meanings from times that predate X-treme sports and *X Files* TV programs. It ventures into the territory of the profane, conjuring up images of things that are just beyond the realm of decency and righteousness. In today's sexually charged culture X means "Look at me, I'm X-rated and X-citing." X is, in a phrase, one of the most provocative signs of contemporary pop culture, characterizing it in a compact yet accurate way.

Its particular design—a cross symbol that has been rotated 45 degrees—reverberates with contradiction and opposition. The cross figure evokes meanings of sacredness, as does its rotation. This is why Christianity is often symbolized with both the cross and X—Christmas is written alternatively as "X-mas." Rotation produces, as does any modification of a form, an opposition, a tension of meaning—in this case, a tension between the sacred and the profane. Writing started out, in fact, as a divine code that was perceived to have magical and supernatural functions. That is why writing was used primarily to record the intentions of the gods. The ancient Egyptians called their writing system hieroglyphic because they used it officially to record hymns and prayers, to register the names and titles of individuals and deities, and to record various community activities—hieroglyphic derives from *hieros*, "holy," and *glyphein,* "to carve." In their origins, most scripts were deemed to have sacred or mystical meanings—for example, the Cretans attributed the origin of writing to Zeus, the Sumerians to Nabu, the Egyptians to Thoth, the Greeks to Hermes, and the list could go on and on. However, at the same time writing was used, by the more mischievous and impish members of ancient cultures, as graffiti code, being used as well to express profane thoughts on city and village walls.

Brand names with the letter X seem to tap into the above reservoir of connotative meanings in a largely unconscious fashion. So too do other kinds of names, such as those that evoke sensory images (Musk, Splash, etc.) or lifestyle images (e.g. Chanel, Nike, etc.). On the other hand,

indexical brand names—e.g. names that identify the geographical location of a company (American Bell, Southern Bell, etc.)—tend to have a
low CI (Beasley *et al.* 2000).

No wonder, then, that brand names are so fiercely protected by
corporations and manufacturers. They are what allow consumers not
only to identify certain goods and distinguish them from those made or
sold by others, but also to relate to them in cultural (connotative) terms.
As Naomi Klein aptly observes, branding became the general practice
among manufacturers of products early on because the market was
starting to be flooded by uniform mass-produced and, thus, indistin-
guishable products: "Competitive branding became a necessity of the
machine age" (Klein 2000: 6). By the early 1950s, it became obvious
that branding was not just a simple strategy for product differentia-
tion, but the very fuel that propelled corporate identity and product
sales. Even the advent of "no-name" products, designed to cut the
retail cost of buying them to the consumer, has had little effect on
the power that branding holds on people. Names such as Nike, Apple,
Body Shop, Calvin Klein, Levi's, etc. are recognized by virtually anyone
living in a modern-day society. As Klein goes on to remark, for such
firms the brand name constitutes "the very fabric of their companies"
(ibid. 16).

In order to decode brand image, it is clearly useful to have a taxonomy
of name-giving strategies, given that the brand name itself is the first critical step in producing an identity for the brand. Most of the names given
to products fall into several main categories. These will be discussed
separately in the remainder of this section.

First, as discussed in the previous chapter, there is the use of the
manufacturer's name (Gucci, Armani, etc.) as a pivotal strategy, which
tends to have a high CI based on meanings that include "artistry," "reliability," "continuity," etc. Internationally recognizable surname brands
include Ford, Kraft, Heinz, Versace, Gillette, Singer, Edison, Firestone,
Dolce and Gabbana, Bally, Boeing, Rolls and Royce, Cinzano, Colgate,
and Porsche (among many others). As shown in Table 3.1, these brand
names are, in effect, eponyms of a particular kind, since they refer to a
person whose name is on the product and is thus perceived as being the
source of the product itself.

Surname brands, like the other brand names, must have an appropriate "phonetic quality," so to speak, otherwise they will likely fail in
the marketplace. This is why a company will change its name or else use
an acronymic name derived from the actual name. For example, the New

Table 3.1 Brand names and their implied meanings

Brand names	Implied meanings
Armani	Giorgio Armani is the "symbol" of Milanese fashion
Bell	Alexander Graham Bell invented the telephone and, thus, no other company is perceived to be more knowledgeable of telephone science
Benetton	The Benetton surname has become synonymous with social activism, concern, etc.
Gerber	Daniel Gerber began selling baby foods through grocery stores in 1928, and thus his products are perceived as being trustworthy (on account of their longevity)
Kraft	Kraft was founded in 1910 and thus has a long tradition of providing good quality

York designer Ralph Lifshitz chose to change his "unpleasant-sounding" name to Ralph Lauren, and went on to create a multi-billion dollar clothing enterprise. Similarly, Pietro Cardino of France modified his Italian name to Pierre Cardin, so as to give it a more appropriate "French sound." The Ikea furniture company was one of the first to use acronymy—the first two letters are taken from the initial letters of the name of its founder *I*ngvar *K*amprad; the third letter comes from the initial letter of Kamprad's family farm called *E*lmtaryd; and the final letter comes from the first letter of the Swedish village of *A*gunnaryd (where the farm is located). Another well-known acronymic brand name is the Minolta Camera Company, which is derived from *M*achine *I*nstrument *O*ptical *Ta*jima (the name of a Japanese wholesale firm run by the founder of Minolta). Sometimes, the acronymic name is designed to produce a distinct meaning of its own. For example, the Telus Communications Company was coined as an acronym of the two words "telecommunications" and "universality"; but the name Telus also communicates the meaning of "tell us." Interestingly, a brand name may sometimes produce an undesired effect. When Vick cough drops entered the German marketplace, the company was bewildered to find that the word *vicks* in German was slang for "sexual intercourse." The company quickly changed its German name to Wicks.

Designer brands require further commentary since they particularly tend to generate a high CI. Denotatively, the surname allows us to identify the actual clothing product we may desire to buy (Armani, Tommy Hilfiger, etc.). But connotatively, the designer's name bestows an aura of craftsmanship and superior quality onto the product—not to mention "fashionableness." The clothing item is thus transformed into the "work" of a fashion artist. It is this second-order level of meaning that makes jeans by Tommy Hilfiger or shirts by Ralph Lauren so appealing.

An interesting case in point is the Evisu jean brand. Marketing research shows that luxury or premium denim jeans are the costliest, not because they are any different from other kinds of jeans, but because they are marketed as unique in style (and their marketing is costly). This is undoubtedly the reason why Evisu, which promotes jeans dyed with vintage equipment in order to give them a unique rich deep shade, is among the costliest on the market. Evisu promotes itself to the fashion "cognoscenti" with a red gull logo, which varies in design from pants to pants, reinforcing the uniqueness of each single pair of jeans. This "individualization" is psychologically powerful, since it provides a means for consumers to claim a stake in promoting their individuality. The surfeit and numbing sameness of goods on the market have conspired to produce a nascent cult of connoisseurship whereby ordinary products, such as the Evisu jeans, have become the symbolic means by which consumers convey individuality. Consumer discernment such as this is now a subtle form of social status climbing. Brands such as Evisu have become the symbolic means through which people can distinguish themselves, replacing membership in organizations (such as religions)—a fact brought out by recent jean brand names such as True Religion and All Saints.

Some brand names refer to a fictitious personality, so as to emphasize the intended connotations through fiction and stylized depiction—e.g. Mr Clean and Aunt Jemima. Mr Clean's name suggests what the product does, at the same time that his muscular body and bald head suggest heroic strength. The Aunt Jemima name is actually a nickname, rather than a fictitious name. The Aunt Jemima pancake mix brand was promoted at the Chicago fair in 1910 by a miller named R. T. Davis who engaged former Kentucky slave Nancy Green, 59, to demonstrate the mix at a griddle outside the barrel. Green was nicknamed "Aunt Jemima" by Davis in order to take advantage of the prejudicial views of the era, which saw older female slaves as "great cooks" with a friendly "aunt-like" disposition. Needless to say, the Aunt Jemima brand has been the target of many debates and justified indignation on the part of concerned African–Americans.

The success of the Aunt Jemima brand spawned a number of imitators, among which one of the most successful is that of Betty Crocker, invented in 1921 by Gold Medal flowers to serve as the face-logo of the company. As Marks (2005: 12) points out, according to a 1945 issue of *Fortune* magazine, this fictitious lady was the second most popular woman in America after Eleanor Roosevelt. As surely as young children buy into fantasy worlds, adults of the era seemed to buy into the Betty Crocker myth—an expert cook, a friend, and a friendly mother figure. Played by various actresses on radio and television, Betty became a true icon of "ideal American womanhood" *c*. 1920–60. In an early example of branding in cultural life, Betty appeared in movies and on television. Her physical image was established in 1936 when her first "portrait" was put out by the company. Her countenance was shaped to have a combination of Caucasian features designed to present the perfect composite of the stay-at-home American woman. Twenty years later a new portrait produced a new image—older and friendlier. Currently, her image has been updated to reflect yet a new image of American womanhood. She now resembles a Latina female and a soccer mom at once. The Betty Crocker "makeover" is a perfect example of how brands must constantly be reshaped to keep in step with the times. Put another way, through revision and updating, a brand can retain its CI.

Another example of "character revision" is that of Mr Peanut, the brand icon of the Planters Company, who has been refashioned in 2004 campaigns to be an active participant in basketball games, dance floors, and other trendy cultural venues, so as to portray him as a fun character in synch with the times. Mr Peanut was born in 1916 as a "little peanut person." Although he still wears a top hat, a monocle, and carries a cane (suggesting the glitz, sophistication, and allure of the dance-club scene of the 1920s), his demeanor has been modified to promote a different kind of lifestyle scene.

Some seemingly fictional brand names are based on real people. For example, Duncan Hines is a character seen on boxes of cake and brownie mix. Most people assume he is a fictitious character. In actual fact, there really existed a Duncan Hines, who was born in Bowling Green, Kentucky, in 1880, becoming widely known for his newspaper columns. Around 1950, Hines agreed to let his name be used for food and kitchen products. Another example is the Wendy character of the Wendy's restaurant chain. Dave Thomas, the founder of the chain, actually named it after his daughter, even though the image on the logo is not a photograph or portrait of his daughter, but rather a stylized version.

A second major naming strategy is to use descriptive words or phrases. Some of these simply link the brand to the manufacturer.

Corporate names such as International Business Machines (IBM), Radio Corporation of America (RCA), and Carnation are cases in point. Related to this strategy is the use of toponymy (place names) to identify where a product, service, or company is located. Well-known toponymic brands include Hitachi (a Japanese coastal city), BankAmerica, Norwich Union, Western Pacific, BSA (Birmingham Small Arms), Bell Canada, and Britannica. The name Toshiba is a syllabic amalgam of the *Tokyo Shibaura* Electronic Company.

Some names are "descriptors." For example, many detergents have names referring to some aspect of nature, so as to reinforce the connection between the product and nature's own "cleaning resources"—e.g. Tide (washing powder), Irish Spring, etc. Other detergent brand names specify the emotional effects that ensue from using them—Cheer, Joy, etc.—or else guarantee some positive outcome—Pledge, Promise, etc. Other examples of descriptor brand names are listed in Table 3.2.

In the category of descriptive names can be added metaphorical names that go beyond mere description to suggest meanings that reach into various kinds of cultural symbolism. As a case in point, take automobiles named after animals—Mustang, Jaguar, Cougar, etc. These are consistent with a long-standing perception of the automobile as a replacement of animals as transporters of people. This is why we still refer to the energy associated with motor vehicle engines in terms of "horse power." The linkage of the two domains, automobiles and animals, reaches as well into other domains of cultural symbolism. It shows up, for example, in the use of animal surnames (Fox, Bear, etc.), in animal narratives told to children where animals represent people, in totemic practices, in naming sports teams (Brisbane Broncos, Detroit Tigers, Leeds Rhinos, Chicago Bears, the Black Cats (Sunderland football team) etc.), in heraldic practices, etc. The gods of many early cultures were conceived as animal figures—Egyptian gods had animal heads, the principal god of the Hindus is Ganesha the elephant, the godhead of the Aztecs was the green-plumed serpent Quetzalcoatl.

Animal car names suggest the qualities of the animals that bear that name—a Jaguar suggests a large and powerful creature, a Cougar a fast and exotic animal, etc. By connotative extension, the driver assumes the physical attributes of the animal. The automobile is a body and thus acts as a protective shell. In the public world of traffic, it is perceived as creating a space around the physical body, which is as inviolable as the body itself. Any transgression against the car body is felt *ipso facto* to be a transgression against the person driving the car. If that person is a jaguar or a cougar, one might be wary to commit any transgression against the car—at least conceptually.

Table 3.2 Brand names with a descriptor function

Brand names	Referents	Implied meanings
Cascade Highland Spring Mountain Dew Surf	Nature	Communicate sensory images connected with nature and its resources
Ford Escape Ford Explorer Ford Maverick Jeep Renegade Land Rover Range Rover	The out-doors	Convey the sense that the vehicles will allow city residents to escape and explore the outdoors, to be "renegades," or to live the "cowboy dream" of freedom from the constraints of civilization
Easy Wipe Lestoil One Wipe Quick Flow Wash 'N Wear	Practical activities	Indicate what a product can do, or indicate that the product is user-friendly, simple, uncomplicated, basic, etc.
Bug Off Close-Up Toothpaste Get Off My Garden Joy No Sweat	Cause and effect	Indicate what can be accomplished with the product, or suggest some emotional outcome (joy, cheer, etc.)
Multicorp PowerAd Powergen Superpower	Authority and power	Elicit a forward-looking, strong, or powerful company image
People's Choice Viewer's Choice	Common people	Indicate that the service is egalitarian, common, and/or friendly
General Electric General Foods	The big picture	Create the image of a company that is all-encompassing and popular
Panasonic Timex	Technology	Convey an image of scientific quality and reliability
Burger King Coronation	Royalty	Imply that the product is fit for royalty

Names that have a primarily descriptive function (Easy On, Quick Flow) or indicate the geographical location of the company (Southern Bell, American Bell) tend to have a low connotative index; metaphorical names that suggest lifestyle or unorthodox activities (Wrangler, Renegade) have a much higher one. "No-name" products do not generate connotative meanings, unless, of course, the no-name product itself has become a brand name. This happened paradoxically to the Italian translation of Naomi Klein's book *No Logo* (2000). So successful was her book in Italy, with its anti-brand message, that the name of the book was itself adopted by a condiment company to name one of its products. The No Logo name became, more specifically, a metaphorical brand name in the sense discussed above.

In actual fact, most descriptive names are tropes (figures of speech) of one kind or other (Andren *et al.* 1978). Many brand names are metaphors. For example, the perfume named Poison, by Christian Dior, is a pure metaphor because, as Wolfe puts it, it evokes a sense of "mystery, alchemy and the archetype of the sorceress" (1989: 3). The metaphorical meanings of *poison* are thus transferred to the product, greatly enhancing its allure.

Brand names, as we saw in the previous chapter, do more than just identify the product. Consider again the case of automobiles, where figurative naming strategies abound. Table 3.3 gives a small sampling.

A large number of brand names are coinages that play on the phonetic qualities of the names themselves. Names such as Kodak, Exxon, and Xerox, for instance, have various phonetic and orthographic qualities that make them stand out. Both Kodak and Xerox are "near-palindromes"— i.e. they are words that can be read almost the same forward and backward—and they are constructed with the "power-sounding" letters "X" and "K." Some names are coined instead to sound foreign. For example, the American video game Atari has a Japanese-sounding name in order, evidently, to associate itself with the positive connotations evoked by Japanese technology.

Sometimes a letter embedded in the name takes on special meanings. Recall, for example, the name Acura, which, as suggested in the previous chapter, is imitative simultaneously of Japanese and Italian words. Other car-makers have used this exact same strategy, coining names ending with the vowel "a" which, given the inbuilt melodious quality of names formed in this way, are probably easier to remember, and additionally, bestow an "Italian" quality onto the perception of the automobile's design. Like Acura, each brand name is an amalgam of two morphemes (meaningful parts): a lexical part that suggests a specific meaning and the "a" ending which has the Italian connotation (Table 3.4).

Table 3.3 Figurative naming strategies for automobiles

Figurative category	Meanings		
Animals	Beetle	=	"small and quick"
	Colt	=	"fast"
	Cougar	=	"the fastest and most powerful"
	Jaguar	=	"sleek, stealthy"
	Mustang	=	"very fast, sexually powerful"
	Pony	=	"young, small, speedy"
	Rabbit	=	"cute and small"
	Ram	=	"strong and tough"
	Taurus	=	"bullish, tough, and strong"
Persons	Cavalier	=	"gentleman, man of honor"
	Escort	=	"bodyguard"
	Mini Clubman	=	"trusty, reliable"
	Protégé	=	"provides protection"
	Sidekick	=	"friend, buddy"
Places indicative of lifestyles	Bonneville	=	"good city life"
	Corsica	=	"exotic island"
	Daytona	=	"outdoor, beach life"
	New Yorker	=	"bustling city life"
	Outback	=	"out of the city, frontier"
	Riviera	=	"French Riviera, chic lifestyle"
	Seville	=	"city of legendary enchantment"
	Sierra	=	"outdoor, expansive"
	Towncar	=	"out on the town"
	Villager	=	"village life"
Music indicative of artistry	Allegro	=	"rapid movement"
	Prelude	=	"musical form originating in the Baroque"
	Sonata	=	"classical music form"
	Tempo	=	"musical pace and rhythm"
Foreign associations	Fiesta	=	"small carnival"
	Grand Prix	=	"European car racing"
	Ka	=	"spirit"
	Le Baron	=	"nobility"
	Le Car	=	"chic French design"
	LeSabre	=	"swordsman"

Table 3.4 Automobile names amalgamating a lexical part with the grammatical morpheme -a

Brand names	Suggested meanings of the lexical parts
Achieva	"achievement," "vivacious"
Acura	"accurate"
Altima	"altitude," "ultimate"
Aurora	"aurora," "dawn"
Corsica	"Corsica" (mystical island)
Elantra	"elegant + mantra"
Festiva	"festive"
Integra	"integral"
Lumina	"luminous"
Maxima	"maximum"
Precidia	"precision," "precedent"
Sentra	"sentry + mantra"
Serenia	"serene"
Sonata	"sonata" (classical music form)
Vectra	"vector" (a quantity possessing magnitude and direction)

The same type of "connotative suggestiveness" is noticeable in a host of brands with names consisting of two or more morphemic parts, each one suggestive of a specific word. The amalgam construction strategy is not limited, of course, to car names. It is found ubiquitously: e.g. brand names such as MaxiLight, SuperFresh, UltraLite, and Fruitopia (= Fruit + Utopia) suggest product "superiority," "excellence," "utopian qualities," etc. Table 3.5 examples such names as given to Viagra-type products.

Brands named with symbols such as letters of the alphabet or with acronyms abound in the marketplace today, for the reasons discussed above with regard to X. Symbolic brands include X-Factor drinks, BVD underwear, CNN, BMW, V-8 vegetable juice, BMX, the Toyota XR Matrix, etc. Abbreviated writing and name-giving was used by the Greeks as early as the fourth century BCE, gradually evolving into a true shorthand code, known as *tachygraphy*. It was the slave Tyro who probably invented the first true shorthand system around 60 BCE (after alphabets had become the norm), apparently for recording the speeches of Cicero (Cherry 1957: 35).

Table 3.5 Viagra-type products with amalgamated names

Brand names	Suggested meanings
AndroGel	"gel to enhance one's quantity of androgen" (a steroid hormone, such as testosterone or androsterone, that controls the development and maintenance of masculine characteristics)
Masculex	"masculine law" (Latin *lex*, "law")
Viga	"vigor"
ViraMax	"maximum virility"

These symbolic strategies are of great interest to both semioticians and linguists because they can be seen to fall under the rubric of what is known as Zipf's Law, after the late Harvard Linguistics Professor George Kingsley Zipf (Zipf 1935, 1949). In a series of statistical studies during the 1930s, Zipf noticed that the shortest words (in number of alphabet characters) were the most frequently used ones in all kinds of written texts—in English these would include words such as "a," "the," "and," and the like. Zipf then went on to generalize his discovery with the notion that languages tend to evolve economically, making progressively greater use of such "compression strategies" as abbreviation, acronymy, and the like: ad = advertisement; NATO = North Atlantic Treaty Organization, laser = light amplification by stimulated emission of radiation, etc. This derived "Principle of Economy" can also be seen in the use of tables, technical and scientific notation systems, indexes, footnotes, bibliographic traditions, etc. All such phenomena validate the underlying implication in Zipf's Law that compression saves effort (Roelcke 2002). The operation of Zipf's Law is particularly evident in how languages have been changing in cyberspace and in SMS messages on mobile telephony, where coinages such as b4 = "before," f2f = "face-to-face," gr8 = "great," h2cus = "hope to see you soon," g2g = "gotta go," etc., have become the norm.

Coining brand names with single letters in them fits in nicely with this general tendency. In a phrase, it speaks to the times. But it does much more than that. Consider the letter X again, which comes from an Egyptian hieroglyph (Driver 1976; Davies 1988; Drucker 1995). As a rotated cross it acts, arguably, on our collective unconscious. It is what Jung called an archetype—symbols that are embedded in the collective unconscious of our species (Stevens 1990). The X was originally a pictograph and thus a symbol associated primarily with priests (Illich and

Sanders 1988; Man 2000). It became an alphabet character later—every alphabet character, in fact, was born as a pictograph. The first alphabetic system emerged in the Middle East around 1000 BCE, and was then transported by the Phoenicians (a people from a territory on the eastern coast of the Mediterranean, located largely in modern-day Lebanon) to Greece. It contained signs for consonant sounds only. When it reached Greece, signs for vowel sounds were added to it, making the Greek system the first full-fledged alphabetic one.

The transition from pictorial to sound-alphabetic representation came about to make writing rapid and efficient. So, for example, instead of drawing the full head of an ox, at first only its bare outline was drawn. This then came to stand for the ox, which, eventually, came to stand for the word for ox (*aleph* in Hebrew). Finally, it came to stand just for the first sound in the word (*a* in *aleph*), which was represented by simply turning the pictograph 180° (and removing any minor details from it). In actual fact, archeological findings suggest that the Phoenician scribes, who wrote from right to left, drew the ox figure sideways (probably because it was quicker for them to do so). The Greeks, who adapted Phoenician letters, generally wrote from left to right, and so turned the A around the other way. Around 500 BCE writing became more standardized and letters stopped changing directions. By that time, the A assumed the upright position it has today.

Alphabetic writing has become the norm in many cultures. But in every alphabetic sign, there is a pictographic history and prehistory built into it similar to the one described for the letter A. We no longer consciously see the visual content of our letters because we are no longer inclined to extract pictorial meaning from them, just phonetic representation. In the case of X, such representation is hardly how we perceive it. What sound does it stand for? In words such as *Xerox* or *xylophone* we actually pronounce it like a Z. In a fascinating book titled *Sign after the X* (2000), Marina Roy has traced the history of this sign, showing that it has had very little to do with phonetics at any period of its history. Here are a few of its traditional meanings:

- any unknown or unnamed factor, thing, or person
- the signature of any illiterate person
- the sign for mistake
- cancellation
- the unknown, especially in mathematics
- the multiplication symbol
- the Roman numeral ten

- a mechanical defect
- on a map a location
- choice on a ballot
- a motion-picture rating
- a symbol for Christ
- the symbol for a kiss
- the symbol for Chronos, the Greek god of Time
- the symbol for planet Saturn in Greek and Roman mythology.

Today, it stands for youth culture (Generation X), adventure comic heroes (X-Men), and erotic movies (X-rated). The Toronto–Lugano research team started collecting the uses of X in brand naming in 2004, uncovering 121 distinct uses in the year 2004, compared to 102 for its next rival, the letter A. Car models made up over half of these uses. Most of these used X or other single letters in combination with other morphemes, especially numeric ones. Alphanumeric names evoke images of technology and cool. Cadillac, for instance, announced a new model with the name CTS in 2001. Acura has also introduced a new line of models with similarly contrived names such as TL, RL, MDX, and RSX. Hyundai's XG300 model and Toyota's XR Matrix are yet other examples of a strategy that allows a brand to tap into the general trends that have been unfolding in the Global Village and, thus, to keep in step with the times.

As a final word on naming strategies, I would like to suggest that the power of the brand name produces a kind of magic spell on the product that is not unlike the sense of magic that the ancients associated with names. From the beginning of time, language has been thought to have special magical powers. This perception is woven into the prayers, formulas, incantations, and litanies of all religions, which are seen as capable (potentially at least) of curing disease, warding off evil, bringing good to oneself, etc. In many early cultures, even knowing the name of a deity was purported to give the knower great power—e.g. in Egyptian mythology, the sorceress Isis tricked the sun god, Ra, into revealing his name and, thus, allowing her to gain power over him and all other gods. In some cultures, the name given to the newborn child is thought to bring with it all the qualities of the previous individuals who shared that name, weaving a sort of magical protective aura on the individual named after them. The brand name also seems to work an unconscious magic on modern-day humans, making them see, for example, products as necessary for success, beauty, adventure, etc., or creating distinctions between better or worse—be it in body, hairstyle, or general lifestyle.

Brand names create belief in products, in the same way that certain words create belief in religions. Brand names are the windows to the modern-day psyche, working their magic on virtually every person in society.

LOGOS

Logos are the pictorial counterparts of brand names. They are true symbols in the semiotic sense—signs standing for referents in culturally specific and historically meaningful ways (Kress 1996). Until the 1970s, logos on clothes were concealed discretely inside a collar or on a pocket. But today, logos such as Ralph Lauren's polo horseman and Lacoste's alligator are suggestive of heraldry. They constitute symbols of "ersatz nobility" that legions of people are eager to wear. The "good hands" of the Allstate Insurance Company, the "rock" of the Prudential Insurance Company, and the "stagecoach" of the Wells Fargo Company tell "condensed stories" of each brand. They are miniature visual narratives. Hands represent "human sentiments" as mirrored by such common expressions as "keeping in touch," "reach out to someone," "you're in good hands," etc.; a rock is a symbol of "solidity," "reliability," and "stability," as reflected in expressions as "solid as a rock," "rock of ages," etc.; and a stagecoach evokes images of American tradition, since it was the means by which mail and various goods were once transported in the US.

Logos generally have a higher CI than do other kinds of branding devices, because they are visual signs steeped in symbolism. Take, as an example, of "logo power," the Nike logo, which is essentially a checkmark.

As a visual sign suggesting speed, it works on several levels, from the iconic to the mythical. At the iconic level, it implies the activity of running at top speed with the Nike shoe; at the mythic level, it taps into the idea of speed as symbolic of power and conquest (such as in the Olympic races). The combination of these two signifying levels creates a perception of the logo, and thus the product, as having a connection to both reality and narrative history. After all, Nike was the goddess of victory. The Nike logo is a classic case of a company gradually simplifying its corporate identity as its fame increases. The company's first logo appeared in 1971, when the word Nike, the Greek goddess of victory, was printed in orange over the outline of a checkmark, the sign of a positive mark. Used as a motif on sports shoes since the 1970s, this checkmark is now so recognizable that the company name itself has became superfluous. The solid corporate logo design check was registered as a trademark in 1995.

The taxonomy of naming strategies discussed above applies equally to the classification of logo-making strategies, and thus requires no further elaboration here. Portrait logos, for example, correspond to the strategy of using the name of a real or fictitious person. The Betty Crocker products show the figure of the fictitious female; Wendy's restaurants display a portrait of Wendy, etc. Descriptive logos correspond to descriptive names and symbolic logos to symbolic names—the logo of the Jaguar automobile is that of the animal; the logo of the Bell Telephone Company consists of a bell, etc. This iconic relation of brand name and logo constitutes, in a phrase, a form of translation or conversion from one type of sign system (the verbal) to another (the nonverbal). The constant in the translation process is the signification system.

Of particular interest to semiotics are the logos that are designed to tap into mythic themes and concepts. Consider the apple logo adopted by the Apple Computer Company.

As discussed in the previous chapter, this logo suggests an "Eve code," derived from the biblical story of Adam and Eve, which revolves around the eating of an apple containing forbidden knowledge. In actual fact, the Hebrew account of the Genesis story tells of a "forbidden" fruit, not specifically of an apple. The representation of this fruit as an apple came about in medieval depictions of the Eden scene, when painters and sculptors became interested in representing the Genesis story artistically. This biblical symbolism of the apple as "forbidden knowledge" continues to reverberate in modern-day culture. This is undoubtedly why the Apple Computer Company has not only named itself with the word Apple, but has also chosen the picture of this fruit as its logo, implying that it, too, will provide forbidden knowledge to those who buy and use its products. Incidentally, the logo shows an apple that has had a bite taken from it, thus reinforcing the link between the logo and the Genesis story by associating the use of Apple computers and products with Eve, the mother of humanity, who took that fateful first bite. The creator of the logo, a man named Rob Janoff of Regis McKenna Advertising, denies any intent to connect the logo to the Genesis story, claiming instead that he put the bite there in order to ensure that the figure was not interpreted as a tomato. Whatever the truth, the bite in the apple evokes the Genesis story nonetheless because we cannot help but interpret signs in symbolic terms.

Consider, as another example, the Playboy logo of a bunny wearing a bow tie. Its ambiguous design opens up at least two connotative chains that reach deeply into unconscious areas of symbolism:

1 rabbit = 'female' = 'highly fertile' = 'sexually active' = 'promiscuous' = etc. but also: a friendly and reassuring animal.

2 bow tie = 'elegance' = 'night club scene' = 'finesse' = etc.

The appeal of this logo is due, arguably, to this dual signification system. By not being able to pin down what the actual meaning of the logo is, we start experiencing it holistically and, thus, not unlike the way we would experience a mythic story. Rabbits evoke archetypal notions of femininity and fertility, which come to consciousness only through reflection. But its symbolism inhabits many other regions of the unconscious. This is why it surfaces in all kinds of stories and fables, from the Easter Bunny and Brer Rabbit to the ever-satirical Bugs Bunny.

Given the power of the logo, it is little wonder that the term "brand" is no longer used today to refer just to a specific product line, but also to the company that manufactures it, to the image that the company wishes to impart of itself and of its products, and to the "personality structure" that is perceived in users of the product. Witness, once more, Coca-Cola: its logo, a simple, but beautiful, calligraphic rendering of the brand name, is probably the most recognizable visual symbol in the entire world today, incorporating all aspects of the brand name (Figure 3.4).

As mentioned in the previous chapter, Coca-Cola was one of the first brands to spread its image throughout society. It did this at first by imprinting its logo on drinking glasses, providing them to diners and other eateries that featured foods meant to be eaten quickly and cheaply. Since then, Coca-Cola has used a simple, yet effective, strategy—adapt its image to shifting trends in lifestyle.

The CI of the Coca-Cola brand is one of the highest recorded by the Toronto–Lugano research team. It spawned over 50 qualitatively distinct connotative meanings from a broad spectrum of 100 subjects in both

Figure 3.4 Coca-Cola (with permission)

cities. This makes it obvious that the Coke co-option strategy, emblematized by its logo, has worked successfully.

Like Coke, the Disney Corporation is also identified with its logo of the cartoon character Mickey Mouse, which became the Disney logo in 1929, when the corporation allowed Mickey Mouse to be reproduced on school slates. A year later Mickey Mouse dolls went into production and throughout the 1930s the Mickey Mouse logo was licensed with huge success. In 1955 *The Mickey Mouse Club* premiered on US network television, further entrenching the Disney brand into the cultural mainstream. Today, Disney toys, TV programs, movies, DVDs, theme parks, and the like have become part of the experience of childhood. But it is the sheer visual impact that remains important for memory.

Visual symbolism is more ancient and, arguably, more essential than its verbal counterpart. Visual forms were used by humans long before the first civilizations. Carvings of animals on roofs and walls, along with sculptures of animals and female figures, go back tens of thousands of years. According to some estimates, the earliest known visual artifact might even be 135,000 years old. It is an animal bone with 70 arcs, bands, and chevrons etched in it. Whether for decorative reasons, to record something, or for some mystical rite, the bone was undoubtedly created to identify something to the eyes long before the invention of alphabets around 1000 BCE (Davenport 1984).

Contemporary logos are not much different from that bone. The technique of promoting products by identifying them with visual signs has been a primary marketing strategy since the turn of the twentieth century. It was (and continues to be) based on the premise that the appeal of a brand increases if it can be literally associated to some distinguishing visual mark. And, it would seem, the more the mark evokes the same kinds of mystical meanings that early tribal carvings, sculptures, and etched bones evoked, the more psychologically effective it is. As the modern marketer has come to realize, the world of modern human beings is a world of mystical images manifesting themselves in many forms and disguises.

A logo is, legally speaking, a name, symbol, or trademark adopted by a manufacturer or service that has been designed for easy and definite recognition. Logos, as mentioned in the previous chapter, started out as trademarks. The shift of name probably came about for legal reasons—trademarks are protected by law because they provide an easy way to determine who makes a certain product, helping consumers identify brands they liked in the past so they can purchase them again. In the US, the first company to use a trademark has certain rights to that trademark. The term "logo," on the other hand, describes the actual design of trademarks and other distinguishing marks used by manufacturers. Logos, too, are highly protected by law.

The Toronto–Lugano team found that the logo designed to represent basic geometrical forms tends to be perceived as much more aesthetically pleasing than any other kind. In an informal study in early 2005, several large classes of students at the University of Toronto were shown a series of pictures and drawings, ranging from simple geometrical figures to complicated abstract expressionist designs. They were asked to choose which ones they thought would be more effective to create logos for new products. Of the over 500 students involved, 423 chose the drawings sketched with circles, squares, triangles, ellipses, etc. in them. This comes as no surprise. Geometrical figures have always been perceived as beautiful and perfect because, as the ancient Greek philosopher Plato (c. 427–347 BCE) pointed out, they are innate. They come as part and parcel of having a human brain. The circle, for example, is a universal symbol of perfection and infinity, probably because it suggests eternal recurrence. Geometry, as the Greeks envisaged it, was all about "ideal forms" such as triangles, circles, and squares. Amazingly, it quickly developed into a science that has allowed us not only to do many practical things, but also to draw inferences about reality that would not have been possible otherwise.

The same geometrical forms were etched on petroglyphs long before the advent of Greek geometry. The bodies of the animals portrayed on rocks by prehistoric members of tribes are typically square, rectangular or circular, and the horns curved and angled. As Plato imagined, there really does seem to be an innate instinct to use the same basic geometric shapes to represent the same kinds of things. Circles and squares are just as likely to be found in doodles and in logos as they are on prehistoric cave walls.

It should thus come as little wonder to find that many of today's most recognizable and memorable logos are based on geometrical forms. A classic example is the Mercedes-Benz logo.

The geometrical simplicity of this logo is truly magnificent, evoking a latent form of mystical symbolism with its three-pointed star representing land, sea, and air inscribed in an eternal circle. A large number of carmakers have adopted similar types of geometrical logos. Kia, for example, has designed a logo consisting of an ellipse encasing its name; and Nissan uses a circle with its name going through it diametrically.

Strategic design in the creation of logos has become so commonplace in the creation of brand image that we hardly notice it any longer at a rational level; we simply experience it at a subconscious one. The Gerber baby bottles (with their logo of a smiling baby) and the Campbell's soup can, for example, have become so familiar that they have even come to emblemize, respectively, infancy and nourishment themselves. Perhaps no other brand illustrates the ability to harness the psychological power of latent mystical meanings than does, again, the Apple Computer Company. Aside from the fact that Mac computers are easy to use and computationally powerful, they are also perceived generally as trendy and "cool." The iMac line—written with a small "i"—constitutes a case in point. The "i," by the way, is both suggestive of lower-case internet style and of words beginning with it—"intelligence," "imagination," "illumination," etc. The design style of the iMacs is sleek and attractive. It makes them unique on the market and sets the whole line of Mac computers into a psychological opposition with IBM computers. In an informal 2001 survey, the Toronto–Lugano research team asked 50 University of Toronto students (25 males and 25 females) to write down their views of IBM computers versus Mac ones in terms of religious, neurological, gender, and a few other anthropomorphic categories that each product purportedly evokes. The student responses were collected and classified. The results revealed that the two brands generated a system of oppositions. By and large, the students classified the two computers in the following terms (only the assessment of two of the male students differed significantly from the classificatory schema shown in Table 3.6).

This was not a scientific study by any means, but it did seem to flesh out differences in signification systems built into each computer brand in a way that is consistent with design and logo differences. Could this be the reason why Macs have been largely replaced by IBMs in the business workplace? Is the IBM an emblem of the largely masculine business

Table 3.6 Oppositional meanings evoked by IBM versus Mac computers

Category	IBM	MAC
Aesthetics	"virile," "macho"	"effeminate," "beautiful"
Career	"business," "science"	"arts," "design"
Gender	"masculine"	"feminine"
Intellect	"rational," "linear"	"imaginative," "associative"
Look	"traditional," "bland"	"cool," "trendy"
Neurology	"left-hemisphered"	"right-hemisphered"
Politics	"right-wing," "conservative"	"left-wing," "liberal"
Religion	"Protestant"	"Catholic"

world, where flair and style are discouraged? These are, of course, rhetorical questions but, as the informal experiment suggested, they are interesting ones.

The modern histories of graphic design and marketing overlap considerably. The reason is, again, an understandable one—marketing a product requires designers literally to imbue the product with visual meaning. It is impossible to advertise "nameless" and "logo-less" products with any degree of persuasion. These influence people's unconscious perception of objects of consumption as necessary accouterments of life. The objective of marketing today is, arguably, to get people to react to brands in ways that parallel how people respond to art and religious symbolism. There are now even websites, such as AdCritic.com, that feature ads and products for their own artistic merit, so that audiences can view them for their aesthetically pleasing qualities alone.

Of course, not all logos are as successful as the ones described in this chapter. Some are dull and largely ineffectual. To be appealing, as the research team found, they should be simple, based on geometric forms, or on mythic traditions, such as animal symbolism. The best logos are exactly like prehistoric carvings and pictograms, which echo with mysticism. Logo designers and marketers are, in a fundamental sense, our modern-day pictographers.

PRODUCT DESIGN

Another way to raise the CI of a brand is through design—of the product itself or of its container. Who does not recognize a Coke bottle, a Campbell's soup can, or other familiar products? These have become so commonplace that they are hardly recognized any longer as designed specifically to promote product familiarity and appeal through the visual channel. They have become true artifacts in the archeological sense— i.e. mementos of cultural lore.

Product design, like the brand name and logo, ensconces brand image in society. Take Coca-Cola again. The contour, hobble-skirted Coke bottle was created in 1915, becoming one of the world's most familiar bottle designs ever. It is now even stored in museums and private collections. Tab-open tops for Coke were introduced during the mid-1960s, at which time the company also introduced its familiar can. Together with the logo on the bottles and cans, the Coca-Cola design has become an icon of contemporary pop culture.

Not all designs have become so broadly familiar or have been created to have such a high CI. Some are meant to be practical. Aerosol cans, easy-to-open detergent bottles with a tough plastic and durable design,

Figure 3.5
The original
Ford Mustang

lightweight containers for carryable products (pills, candies, etc.), and packages with images that show how to open or close a bag are all examples of designs that have a high practicality in their form (Hine 1995). However, for most brands, design is intended to do much more. For example, the shape, size, and distinctive features of automobiles are not only identifiers of car make, but also a visual coding of the signification system that the manufacturer intends to build into a specific model of automobile. Take, as a classic case in point, Ford's Mustang model, which was introduced on the market in 1964 (Figure 3.5). More than 100,000 Ford Mustangs were sold during the first four months, making it Ford's best early sales success since the introduction of its Model T. The Mustang's design as a quasi-sports car, for the young (or young-at-heart), was indisputably the key to its success.

Marketed as a low-price, high-style car, the Mustang appealed instantly to a large segment of people, imparting a sense of "car artistry" that was associated only with luxury cars. And it was intended to attract men and women equally. Its design included elegant, narrow bumpers instead of the large ones popular at the time and delicate grillwork that would jut out at the top and slant back at the bottom to give the car a forward-thrusting look. Visual interest was added by the air scoops on its sides to cool the rear brakes. Its hefty logo of a galloping horse adorned the grill, as on a Maserati, becoming a veritable icon of pop culture.

The name and car design matched perfectly—a "mustang," although small, is a powerful animal, as is the car; a mustang is a wild horse, as were the youths of the era at the threshold of the counterculture movement, etc.

On the other hand, the 1957 Cadillac El Dorado was designed to evoke a different signification system through both its name and form. The term El Dorado alludes to a magical city of the New World, often thought to be in the northern part of South America, fabled for

Figure 3.6
The original
Cadillac
El Dorado

its great wealth of gold and precious jewels. In its convertible design, the automobile epitomized the large cars of America's "El Dorado" period, also known as the "American Dream" era, with their large tail fins and expansive bodies (Figure 3.6). Although such features did little for the performance of the vehicles, consumers loved the look, and demanded fins of increasing size until the late 1960s.

The spacious design of the automobile and its "bounteous" look were clearly designed to bespeak of luxury, extravagance, and opulence. Driving an El Dorado implied having found the wealth of the fabled place. Design is especially critical in the creation of signification systems for all kinds of lifestyle products. Take, as another example, Absolut Vodka. With its Absolute Ritts campaign of the late 1990s, the brand showcased a picture of the vodka bottle with the silhouette of a nude female body inside it. The name Ritts referred to the well-known photographer Herb Ritts, and the bottle design was made to emulate his own photographs, which were marked by a high degree of sensuality. But the sensuality was tempered by the cool blue background of the sky against which the bottle was cast, creating a "sensory tension" in the viewer, suggestive of sexual arousal.

Strategic design is also a large part of the fascination associated with buying perfume and cologne products. Most of the bottle designs of the "high-class" ones range in style from the Gothic and neoclassical to the modern and postmodern. Chanel and Houbigant bottles are hardly "throw-aways." They have the same "timeless" look about them that precious artifacts or artworks have. The Toronto–Lugano research found, in fact, that they are kept for long periods of time by consumers. Subjects were asked if they kept certain types of perfume bottles longer than others that could be deemed to be more "discardable." The findings confirmed that people do, indeed, keep them longer. Of 24 subjects who were chosen to be interviewed—all of them selected because they

identified themselves as consumers of Chanel perfume products—
19 admitted to holding on to the bottles longer by simply not finishing
their contents quickly, keeping them from half to three-quarters empty
in their bathrooms or boudoirs in plain view.

As a practical illustration of the "lure of the bottle," consider the pitch-
dark, elliptically shaped Drakkar Noir cologne bottle (by Guy Laroche).
A recent ad for the brand pictured a masculine hand holding the
bottle tightly, at the same time that a feminine hand holds his hand, just
as tightly.

First, note that the color of the bottle and the name of the cologne
are iconic counterparts. The bottle has a black color, connoting fear,
night, and the occult—a design feature that expresses in visual form the
meaning of the name *Noir* (French for "black"). The sepulchral name,
Drakkar, is also congruous with the bottle's design at a connotative level,
reinforcing the idea that something scary, but nevertheless desirous, may
happen by splashing on the cologne. The guttural Drakkar name is
suggestive phonetically of Dracula, the deadly vampire who, in countless representations, mesmerized his sexual prey with a mere glance.
Sexual imagery is implicit in the entire visual text, by the way; and the
phallic symbolism is unmistakable. The connotative chain that the ad,
along with bottle design and name, establishes is thus the following one:

> darkness = night = something desirable = Dracula legend =
> sexuality = phallicism = etc.

Needless to say, other connotative chains can also be envisioned,
probably because the vampire figure has come to symbolize other things.
One of these is the breaking of taboos. The figure of Dracula challenges
authority, putting forward a fine line between passion and power, and
resuscitating the mythical search for eternal youth and immortality.
Stoker's Dracula (in the original novel of 1897) was the embodiment of
evil, but the Dracula that finds its way into modern-day representations
has evolved into a much more ambivalent creature—a reflection of the
blurring of the boundaries between Good and Evil in pop culture.
Moreover, the word "Drakkar" actually has a Viking origin, referring to
the long ship or dragon ship of Viking legend—a warship designed to
carry the virtual warriors on their raids over a millennium ago. It is not
possible to ascertain whether the brand has intentionally attempted to
play on this ambiguity of Dracula and Viking virility. Nevertheless, the
phonetic quality of the word itself unmistakably suggests Viking-like
strength.

The above discussion encapsulates the findings of the Toronto–Lugano
research team, which showed the ad to 30 subjects in the year 2003,

indicating that the brand has a high CI. Consider, as another example of bottle design with a high CI, the Versus cologne product that was advertised extensively in magazines in the late 1990s and early 2000s. The bottle has a prominent V-shape figure, conveying at an iconic level the association between the cologne's name, Versus, and its manufacturer, Versace.

But the word Versus connotes much more at another level—it connotes "opposition" and "violation." The V-shape can also be seen to constitute a design feature of the bottle that mirrors this signification system, since it connotes "indentation," "cleft," "fissure." The Versace company promoted this signification system with advertising images of affluent, young males who appeared to be prototypes of what urban professional males aspired to look like during leisure hours—hours devoted presumably to mate selection or sexual gratification generally. The design of the Versus bottle can thus be construed to suggest that young men can cross over, symbolically, from the work world to the leisure world—worlds that are in opposition—by dashing on the cologne. The former world is suggestive of the realm of Apollo—the god of male beauty and of the fine arts—and the latter the realm of Dionysus—the god of wine, representing the irrational, undisciplined, and orgiastic side of the male psyche. In this interpretive frame, Versus can be seen to be the olfactory means by which a modern-day Apollo can become his Dionysian self. This mythic interpretation is strengthened by the fact that the V-shape of the bottle design "points downward," suggesting (indexically) the Dionysian underworld of physical desire.

The dark-blue color of the bottle can also be tied to this line of interpretation. Blue is the symbol of masculinity, as pink is that of femininity. The dark-blue tones of the bottle invite the male viewer to enter the dark underworld where his base, primal urges can be released and satisfied. The V-shape intaglio is, in fact, suggestive of an "opening" into this underworld, a crevice that opens up below a Dionysian world of lust and self-indulgence. It is also suggestive of female genitalia—presumably the object of male desire.

But, there are other interpretive paths that the bottle design opens up. One can ask, in fact, whether the object of sexual desire is really the "opposite" of female genital symbolism, as the name Versus suggests implicitly. In other words, does the cologne allow the men to descend even further into deeply hidden homosexual desires?

Whether or not the two interpretations put forward here are correct in any real sense, is beside the point. The point I really wish to make is that both are seemingly possible (or at least plausible), because the design features of the bottle and its logo generate an entangled web of ambiguous sexual connotations. In sum, the Versus bottle is a miniature work of art, with its allusion to "oppositional" tendencies in the male psyche.

Aware of the power of design in the creation of a signification system for a product, the makers of Salem cigarettes attempted, in the late 1990s, to win over young smokers by creating a trendier image for its cigarette brand, while at the same time striving to avoid the backlash from society that has beset the tobacco industry in the last few decades. Using an abstract style to design the cigarette package, akin to that employed by symbolist or expressionist painters, Salem marketers tested the new-look product with an ingenious market campaign. The company mailed out a sample package along with four gift packages—a box of peppermint tea, a container of Chinese fortune cookies, a bottle of mint-scented massage gel, and finally a candle. Each package—on which a small notice contained the message "Mailing restricted to smokers 21 years of age or older"—came with a coupon for a free pack of cigarettes. The package's symbolist design, along with the occult nature of the gifts, imparted a mystical aura to the cigarettes, mirroring a "New Age" strain present in youth culture that Salem attempted to tap into. Salem also touched up its "S" logo and package typeface to reflect a New Age look, with Gothic-looking fonts and shapes. It is no coincidence that the name of the brand itself is suggestive of the occult. The Salem witchcraft trials—the result of the largest witch hunt in American history— were held in 1692 in Salem, a town in the Massachusetts Bay colony. Nineteen people, both men and women, were convicted and hanged as witches. About 150 other people were imprisoned on the witchcraft charges. The Salem trials resulted in the last witchcraft executions in America.

Similarly, the Brown & Williamson Tobacco Company has revamped the package design of its Kool brand of cigarettes, which comes in flavors as well—Caribbean Chill, Midnight Berry, Mocha Taboo, and Mintrigue—all with their own design variations according to name. The corners of the packages are round, rather than rectangular—a trend probably started by Apple computers with their iBook and iMac product lines. Roundness is a signifier of elegance and femininity, as experiments by Gestalt psychologists and semioticians have shown (e.g. Danesi 1998). Reinforcing this signification system is the addition of vivid colors to the boxes and the fact that the pack opens like a book to reveal marketing copy entreating smokers into a world of mystery.

In modern consumerist cultures, it is difficult indeed to determine what is art and what is not, given the spread of strategic product design. Already in 1913, the French–American artist Marcel Duchamp (1887– 1968) produced an upside-down but otherwise unaltered Bicycle Wheel, asserting that it (or any other everyday object) constituted a sculpture if an artist declared it to be so. Duchamp soon followed the bicycle wheel with a bottle rack, snow shovel, and most notoriously, a urinal. The attitude of Duchamp and other members of the so-called Dada movement who shared his views about art reemerged in the early 1960s through an international group of artists calling themselves Fluxus, who sought to erode the barriers between art and life and allow randomness and chance to guide their work.

The movement that brought consumer objects into the realm of "art" was the *pop art* (short for *populist art*) one, which started after World War II. It was inspired by the ingenuity of design employed to manufacture brand products. For pop artists, the factory, the supermarket, and the garbage can became their art school. Despite its apparent absurdity as an "art movement," many people loved pop art, no matter how controversial or crass it appeared to be. The pop art movement gained momentum in the late 1950s, when painters such as Robert Rauschenberg (1925–) and Jasper Johns (1930–) strove to close the gap between traditional art forms and the mass-produced objects that characterized life in consumerist cultures. Rauschenberg constructed collages from household objects such as quilts and pillows; Johns from American flags and bull's-eye targets. Pop artists also appropriated the techniques of mass production. Rauschenberg and Johns had already abandoned individual, titled paintings in favor of large series of works, all depicting the same objects. In the early 1960s, the American Andy Warhol (1928–87) carried their idea a step further by adopting the mass-production technique of silk-screening, turning out hundreds of identical prints of Coca-Cola bottles, Campbell's soup cans, and other familiar objects, including identical three-dimensional Brillo boxes. Perhaps its most important impact has been on the business world itself, where it is seen as a mirror of changing pop-culture aesthetics. The design of the Campbell's soup can, for example, underwent a major change in 1994, probably because it had become so trivialized by the Warhol representation. At the bottom of the red-and-white can there is now a picture of the soup to be found within the container. This has created a new signification system for the product, which, before the change, was losing customer loyalty and was thus in need, literally, of a "face lift."

In a way, then, visual image seems to be the paramount factor in the construction of brands, especially the way that branding impacts on product design and logos that raise the profile of the brand. But this is by no means the end of the discussion. Brands are frequently sustained by lengthy advertising campaigns; these often consist of characters and recurrent themes, but they are usually highly reliant on linguistic devices such as straplines, slogans, and jingles. Clearly, the image in brand management is of immense importance. However, it would be wrong to downgrade the role of words in brands' multimodal bearing. This will be the main theme of the next chapter.

4

BRAND TEXTUALITY

Ideally, advertising aims at the goal of a programmed harmony among all human impulses and aspirations and endeavors. Using handicraft methods, it stretches out toward the ultimate electronic goal of a collective consciousness.

Marshall McLuhan (1911–80)

In *Just So Stories for Little Children* (1902), Rudyard Kipling wrote stories for children to explain natural phenomena in a fanciful yet compelling way—e.g. "How the Leopard Got Its Spots." The expression "Just-So story" crystallized shortly thereafter as a widely used one in reference to any artfully contrived explanation or story, even if it has little basis in fact. It is certainly an apt one in reference to modern-day advertising, which is, essentially, the art of the Just-So story. Without such stories, brand images would evanesce virtually overnight.

This chapter will look at how brand image is sustained and spread. Through ad campaigns that are implanted on recurrent themes, characters, slogans, jingles, and images of specific types, the signification system that defines brand image is given a textual form. The term *text*, as it is used in semiotic theory, means a "putting together" of signifying elements (words, sounds, images, etc.) to produce a meaningful message. For instance, in the Canadian milk advertising campaign, "Drink milk, love life!" of the late 1990s, the choral "Ode to Joy" section of the fourth movement of Ludwig van Beethoven's Ninth Symphony was used to suggest a sense of joy that can be attained by drinking milk. The use of Beethoven's music was intended, clearly, to emphasize the uplifting qualities of fresh milk through the jubilant feeling evoked by the music. In a word, it was given textual form. Advertising textuality is the fifth main strategy in the development and ensconcement of brand identity delineated in the previous chapter.

TEXTUALITY

The signification systems that are established through brand names, logos, and product design constitute the "referential systems" upon which advertisers create ad texts to display them in various media (print, radio, television, etc.). The form they are given in advertising campaigns can be called their "textuality." This refers to the customary manner in which the brands construct their advertising messages. As an example of how textuality is established, consider the ad campaigns that Budweiser has mounted since 2000. These are all designed to be in synch with the comedic styles of the day:

- 2000: Movie dog Rex motivates himself with an imagined chase of a Budweiser beer truck, which ends in a blind leap over a hedge, face first, into a packed van.
- 2001: Cedric the Entertainer's dream date goes awry when his shaken-up bottle of Bud Light spews on his date—a commercial that is in line with what some call "nerdy" humor in which a "nerd" displays his lack of social skills.
- 2002: A wife lures her husband to a bedroom with the promise of Bud Light. He dives for the beer and slides out of a window on their satin sheets.
- 2003: A football team turns to a zebra referee to review a call—a skit in obvious imitation of "sports buffoonery" that was popular in movies of the era as well.
- 2004: A yuppie's pedigreed pooch fetches him a Bud Light, biting his crotch to get some of it—in line with the moronic humor of sitcoms such as *South Park* and others.

Humor and irony were the strategic elements of the scripts constructed by Budweiser—elements that reinforced the image of the beer as a symbol of a carefree lifestyle and imitative of sitcom-style comedy.

A different kind of textuality is used, generally speaking, for the advertising of beauty and cosmetic products. Consider, for instance, the erotic connotations built into advertising campaigns for Living Proof Cream Hidracel moisturizer during the late 1990s and early 2000s (Berger 2000: 59–60). The verbal part of the ad texts promised that the cream would help women remain young and avoid "drying up" like prunes. The phrase "a peach juicy" in the text was an interpretive key to the brand's signification system. Having peach-like skin, by "moistening" it evoked, as Berger points out, images of female genitalia. The same kind of textuality was built into the promotion of Pango Peach, a lipstick brand introduced by Revlon in 1960. Ads promoting the product have ever since described its use in highly erotic ways (Berger 2000: 61) with expressions such as "pink with pleasure," "a volcano of color," "fullripe peach," "succulent on your lips," "sizzling on your fingertips," etc. These are suggestive, clearly, of female sexual organs and sexual activities, at the same time that they refer denotatively to the gustatory reactions that ensue from eating a peach.

The peach color of the products in the ads produces a tactile sensation in viewers. One can almost "feel" the peach in one's hands. This indirect stimulation of a sensation is known as "synesthesia." Synesthesia connects the viewer to the ad text in a sensory Just-So way. As Lindstrom (2005) argues, the most successful advertising strategies are those that integrate sensory processes synesthetically. He points out, for instance, that Kellogg's trademarked crunchy sound and feel of eating cornflakes was created in sound laboratories. Aware of its synesthetic qualities, the company patented it in the same way that it patented its recipe and logo.

The Toronto–Lugano research team collected nearly 2,000 ads for lifestyle products taken from 100 magazines published in North America and Europe in 2002 to assay if synesthesia was a widespread textual strategy. As it turned out, over 900 were determined to have a synesthetic textuality built into them, which is a significantly high number. Table 4.1 is an illustrative sampling of the ads. Under the column labeled "synesthetic quality" are paraphrases of the reactions that a group of five subjects said they felt as they viewed the ads.

Synesthetic textuality allows viewers to indulge in an ersatz form of voyeurism, since it stimulates sensory reactions through viewing. It thus imparts sensations that the product is supposed to stimulate in a·real way (Barthes 1977). The surface text, which identifies a product and presents a situation or image, unfolds in the mind as an action sequence. The synesthetic effect occurs not from individual elements in the surface text, but in their relationships to each other. Thus, the sensation of cold comes across not from viewing the ice cube by itself, but from observing its placement on the neck. The level at which these relationships generate sensations and other kinds of meanings is commonly referred to as the "subtext." Another kind of relationship occurs "outside the text." The erotic sensation derived from viewing the lips in the ad described above come not from the nature of lips themselves, but from their erotic

Table 4.1 Synesthetic qualities of certain ads

Brand	Ad text	Synesthetic quality
Chambord champagne	A man is about to kiss an attractive young woman whose head is slightly askew in the direction of the viewer. She is looking directly at the viewer, as she touches the bottom of a champagne-filled glass. A spotlight falls gently on her eyes and lips, which are colored with the same auburn color of the champagne.	The erotic taste of female lips
Davidoff Cool Water (eau de toilette for men)	A nude young man, seen from the waist up, is splashing in a pool of water. The expression on his face is that of someone reacting ecstatically to the feel of cool water on his body.	The sensation of cool water on the skin
Rémy Martin cognac	A beautiful young woman exposes her neck by tilting her head slightly to the side. A handsome man behind her touches her neck with an ice cube, as it melts, dripping all over her neck and chest area. The color of the melted water is that of the cognac.	The cold sensation of an ice cube on one's neck in contrast to a hot sensation linked to the reddish color of the cognac
Skyy vodka	A man dressed in a black satin suit is sitting in a leather armchair. A woman dressed in a low-cut leather dress is sitting on him, facing him with her knees on his crotch and touching his face with silk gloves. She is about to kiss him as he lies still.	The feel of leather, satin, and silk

connotations as portrayed in all kinds of other texts. Allusions of this kind are considered to be elements of "intertextuality" (Eco 1979, 1990; Bernardelli 1997; Allen 2000; Beard 2001).

Textuality can also be evaluated in terms of the notion of connotative index, since the ad campaigns are really vehicles for delivering signification systems along with names and logos. The Toronto–Lugano team found that synesthetic texts have, surprisingly, only an average CI when compared to the type of textuality manifested by high-couture cosmetic brands such as Chanel. The average number of connotations recorded for synesthetic texts was from four to five, most of which provided descriptive detail on the type of sensation evoked by the texts. On the other hand, the surrealistic texts created for Chanel products generated so many qualitatively distinct interpretations that the research team decided not to count them.

To get a sense of why these ads are so obscure, consider a classic Coco Chanel ad campaign of the 1990s, which showed a young woman (French singer, Vanessa Paradis) dressed up to resemble a bird, with a tail. She had a rope tied around her left ankle, and was dressed in erotic clothing (footless fishnet tights, long black gloves, etc.). The number of subtextual meanings suggested by the text is unquantifiable. One possible interpretation is suggested by the Coco name itself, which was the nickname of the late founder of Chanel, Gabrielle Bonheur Chanel. Its phonetic quality suggests onomatopoeically the sound that some birds are perceived to make. And at the time, Coco was also an abbreviation for "cocaine," which is not only a narcotic, but also an aphrodisiacal intoxicant. Together with the visual image, the text seems to suggest that the perfume will allow females to be "sexually wild" and "uninhibited." Reinforcing this interpretation was a ravenous, "bird-like" expression on the model's face. The metaphorical association of the female figure to a bird is a deeply embedded one in our culture. In American slang, for example, a young woman is sometimes called a "chick"; in British slang, some men refer to women as "birds." The English expressions "stuffing a bird" and "getting tail" mean "to have sex with a woman"; but it is not just in English that this applies: the same is true of expressions in other languages, such as German. The oversized Coco bottle, with its vivid amber color, juxtaposed against the dark background, was highly suggestive of fire and flames, and, thus, reinforced the sexual sense of "burning desire" communicated overall by the textuality of the ad.

But the above interpretation is only one of many more. Another plausible interpretation of the ad could also be that of women as "pets" adored, pampered, and "maintained" (enslaved) by men for sexual amusement and gratification. This interpretation is reinforced by the fact that the woman in the ads was tied to a rope, making her escape from the scene impossible. Another possible interpretative line of reasoning was that of "woman-as-sexual-slave." The rope tied around her ankle had a spermatozoid shape, although it was colored red—a symbol of female sexuality. The ambiguity of the rope's meaning is brought out further by the fact that the one who held the rope could not be seen—he or she was just beyond the contours of the print space. Was the holder of the rope—the source of her enslavement—a man, the dark forces of nature, or even the woman herself?

The woman in the ads was barefoot, which is suggestive of the female's biological role as "mother" and as an "earth-bearer." The woman held a bottle of Coco next to her face and breast, as she would a child. And while the woman's bare back, shoulders, and scanty attire produced erotic imagery, her slightly turned bodily orientation, concealing her private parts, was suggestive of modesty. The juxtaposition of eroticism and modesty gave the woman in the ads great allure.

Another interpretation of the ad was that of a surrealistic dream world. This was evoked by the fact that the woman was surrounded by a dark void, and that she seemed to appear mysteriously "out of nothingness," as in a dream. Was she a figment of the libidinous imagination? In sum, there is no end to the meaning one can extract from the ad. In a real sense, the ad was a work of surrealist art—the art form that attempts to express the workings of the subconscious through fantastic imagery and the incongruous juxtaposition of subject matter. As Judith Williamson (1996) has astutely pointed out, texts such as Coco Chanel one constitute "surrealist puzzles."

Surrealism is a common technique in many ads. As Bachand (1992: 5) remarks, it is a technique that "has been and still is a great inspiration to advertisers." In general, ads for many types of perfume, clothes, alcoholic beverages, and other lifestyle products are designed to produce either a synesthetic reaction, to pose surrealist puzzles, or to generate mythic images. And although the details of the ads will change, in line with changing social trends, the subtext tends to remain the same, since it is the level at which the signification system of a brand is embedded. What changes is the style of presentation and the elements used to construct the text.

Budweiser has been particularly adept at changing with the times. Budweiser ads of the late 1990s "spoke" to average young males and to the importance of bonding for this age group. They showed males hanging out together, performing bizarre male bonding rituals (burping, picking noses, watching TV sports programs together, etc.), and generally conveying culturally biased notions of masculinity. The details of the scripts and the humor employed by the characters changed constantly, but the subtext remained the same. Its general meaning was: "You're one of the guys, bud."

Another company that has always fashioned its image to be *au courant* is Calvin Klein. An early 2000 ad campaign by Calvin Klein for its Contradiction for Men line of cologne brought this out emphatically. One of the ads showed a black-and-white photograph of a young man, dressed in a leather jacket, who could be seen lovingly embracing and kissing a naked male child. The child seemed satisfied and happy; he also could be seen wearing a silver-steel watch rather conspicuously. The bottle—an objet d'art resembling a modern monolithic sculpture—was placed in the right-hand corner.

There were many "contradictions" built into this ad—as many as there are in perceptions of the male gender. First, there is the obvious one of the man assuming the traditional role assigned to females—caring lovingly for the baby, and thus showing his feelings overtly. But there is also a nature vs. culture dimension to the ad, as suggested by the fact that the baby was naked (a natural state) but the man was clothed in a leather jacket (a cultural state). The synesthetic textuality to the ad, induced by the leather touching naked skin, and by the fact that the man was wearing a watch made of silver or steel, reinforced this nature vs. culture interpretation. Creating contradictions has always been a part of the textuality of Calvin Klein ads. From early campaigns showing models in statuesque poses and in gardens of various types, Calvin Klein has tried to bring out the contradictions of social life—which is at odds with nature. The subtext is, in all likelihood, that perfumes and colognes are the sensory means by which these contradictions can be resolved.

LANGUAGE DEVICES

Ad texts are elaborations of the signification systems built into brand names and logos. For example, TV commercials for the Towncar and the New Yorker in the late 1990s showed the automobile in a large city environment with fashionably dressed drivers; those for Cougar and Mustang, on the other hand, showed the car driven in the outdoors, speeding by freely, unencumbered by buildings and other cars; commercials for the Sonata and Prelude cars typically featured a classical music soundtrack and showed the car being driven by "high class" personages.

Ad textuality is essentially "bimodal," since most ads are constructed with verbal and nonverbal devices. The former will be discussed in this section and the latter in the section below. The catalogue of verbal devices is a long one. Following is a discussion of the seven main ones (see also Dyer 1982: 151–82; Myers 1994; Goddard 1998; Hermerén 1999; Ries and Ries 2002: 123–5).

One of the most effective of all the verbal strategies is the use of slogans and jingles, which are designed to put the signification system (literally) of a brand into words: "Have a great day at McDonald's"; "Drink Milk, Love Life." Formulas of this type are constructions that incorporate the seven other kinds of linguistic strategies in some way. In a fundamental sense, all linguistic forms in advertising are essentially slogans.

Table 4.2 The use of the imperative in ads

Brand	Ad text	Caption/headline
Disaronno Originale (Amaretto)	A photograph on a matchbox of a sexy woman hugging a man who has his lips near her neck is shown. A lit match at the bottom of the page is followed by the slogan.	Light a fire!
Marlboro cigarettes	A cowboy is seen on a horse pulling another horse with no rider on it.	Come to Marlboro country!
Tabù (spray cologne by Dana)	The back of a nude woman is shown as she holds the top of her head with her hand, revealing a partially exposed breast.	If you dare (may cause increased heart rate)!
Tango Twist (Nordstrom)	A perfume bottle with rose petals all around it and a red necklace twisted around its opener is showcased.	Reinvent seduction!
Virginia Slims	A woman is laughing while holding a cigarette in "feminine style," pointing it upwards.	Do the woman thing!

The two slogans used above are in the imperative form. This is, in fact, a major strategy. Slogans in the imperative constitute commands or statements of advice coming from an unseen authoritative source: "Have yourself a Bud"; "Drink Coke"; etc. The imperative impels people to accept the statement as de facto authoritative—since from birth we have been accustomed to process the imperative tense as the language appropriate to such authority figures as parents ("Don't touch that"), teachers ("Do your homework"), clerics ("Love thy neighbor"), law enforcers ("Do not break driving speed limits"), etc. The same kind of "authoritativeness" is imparted by the slogans used in captions and headlines. Table 4.2 describes several magazine ads that were compiled by the Toronto–Lugano team in 2002.

It is relevant to note that each imperative statement is really a slogan that is imbued with cultural nuances. The Virginia Slims statement suggests by innuendo that: smoking a cigarette = female power and liberation. The same innuendo can be detected in all kinds of Virginia Slims ads:

> I look temptation right in the eye and then I make my own decision: Virginia Slims. Find Your Voice! (2002)

I know that I'm very complicated. I like it that way: Virginia
Slims! (2003–4)

This was, of course, the signification system on which the Virginia
Slims brand was founded. From the outset, the brand has attempted to
emphasize that smoking, once considered a "male thing," has empow-
ered females, allowing them a symbolic means from which to declare
their independence from social patriarchy. The history of the Virginia
Slims brand constitutes, in effect, "the brand's version of women's
liberation." For women to smoke "their own brand" of cigarette has
always been promoted by Virginia Slims as a subversive social act, thus
tapping into the history of smoking itself which shows, in fact, that
smoking has always been perceived symbolically. As Richard Klein
(1993) has argued in his interesting book, *Cigarettes Are Sublime*, cigarettes
have always had some connection to sex and gender, or to something
that is erotically, socially, or intellectually appealing. Musicians smoke;
intellectuals smoke; artists smoke. Smoking is a symbol of sexuality,
power, self-control. Smoking is, as Virginia Slims clearly knows, both
a subversive and a tantalizing activity allowing women to do their own
thing.

The imperative is not only used to evoke a sense of authoritativeness,
but also friendly advice, recommendation, etc. An analysis of 250 ads by
the Toronto–Lugano research team (published between 2003 and 2005)
showed that 112 of them used the imperative not only as a form of
authority, but also of advice of various kinds. The following verb forms
occurred in a considerable number of the 112 ads:

Be . . .
Bring . . .
Come . . .
Do . . .
Drink . . .
Eat . . .
Explore . . .
Find . . .
Give . . .
Go . . .
Have a . . .
Imagine . . .
Join . . .
Keep . . .
Let . . .

Look . . .
Make . . .
Open . . .
See . . .
Stay . . .
Take . . .
Try . . .

Needless to say, not all verbs are in the imperative. The actual tense and mood of the verb allows the text to refer to the past, present, or future, and thus bestow upon the brand image connotations of tradition, currentness, or futurity, as the case may be. A 2005 campaign by the Ontario government in Canada consisted of putting a series of posters on subway walls showing images of the countryside and of recreational areas in the province. Each poster had one participial on it that captured both the nature of an activity and the desirable effects it produces— "Exhilarating," "Refreshing," "Relaxing," etc.

A third main linguistic strategy is the use of speech formulas of various kinds to transform meaningless statements about products into Just-So ones: "Triumph has a bra for the way you are"; "A Volkswagen is a Volkswagen"; etc. In a sales pitch for its newspaper, the *New York Times* created the following headline during the early 1980s:

Clarity begins at home
with the home delivery of
the *New York Times*

The line "Clarity begins at home" is an obvious modification of the proverb "Charity begins at home." This clever use of proverbial phraseology imparts "folk wisdom" meanings to the *New York Times*. Folk wisdom is the generic term for the "grass-roots" insights on life and human behavior transmitted in a culture through its proverbs, aphorisms, and other linguistic formulas. Although some of these may pass in and out of written literature and may cross over from oral tradition, an essential trait of such insights is their broad appeal, being perceived intuitively as timeless and revealing hidden truths.

A fourth major strategy is the use of poetic devices such as alliteration, rhyme, rhythm, and metaphor. These increase the likelihood that a brand name will be remembered: "The Superfree sensation"; "Guinness is good for you"; "Toys for tots"; etc. (Tash 1979). An ad designed to attract business in the *New York Times* in 1977 began as follows:

Franchisers
Find
Franchisees
Fast

The alliteration of "F" in the ad is both effective as a mnemonic device and as a tongue-twisting ploy that engages readers in a pleasant and interesting way, forcing them to take notice. A 2002 Burger King ad also used the alliteration of this sound with its "Fiery Fries" ad campaign, reinforcing the alliteration visually by showcasing a French fry topped with ketchup, making it look like the substance used to produce a flame on a match. Also, the sequence of a trisyllabic word ("fiery") followed by a monosyllabic one ("fries") creates a catchy rhythm, further enhancing the poetic force of the slogan.

Sometimes the alliteration is lexical, i.e. it occurs at the word level through the repetition of the same word, but with a different meaning. For example, in the 1970s, Sudden Beauty used the following headline in a variety of magazine ads (Tash 1979):

How to make up
Without make-up!

Such poetic license is not only appealing, it is memorable because it conveys its message through rhyme, rhythm, and repetition. The use of formulas is also a common rhetorical strategy. A 2002 ad for Visa Gold, for example, went like this:

He who has the gold makes the rules!

This type of formula is imbued with "authoritativeness" by virtue of the fact that it has been constructed in the form of an aphorism or proverb —i.e. in the form of a statement that is designed to illustrate something as a basic truth or a practical precept, implying depth of content. It is also a clever play on the expression "the golden rule"—the precept that people should do to others as they would have others do to them.

At other times an expression is altered in a strategic way. An example of this was TWA's extremely successful ad campaign of the 1970s, which used the following headline (Tash 1979: 229):

TWA's
Spring Sale
on the Rockies

The expression "on the Rockies" can, of course, be read as meaning literally "on the Rocky Mountains" (the place where TWA would fly someone). Additionally, it can be construed as a slight modification of the idiomatic expression "on the rocks" ("with ice" as in "I'll have my Martini on the rocks"). The latter sense was reinforced by the pictorial part the ads, which generally showed skiers with their skis and poles, hanging out in a bar waiting for their drinks "on the Rockies."

A fifth major strategy is the strategic avoidance of any language whatsoever, suggesting, by implication, that the product speaks for itself. As Dyer (1982: 170) puts it, the absence of language in certain ad texts "has the effect of making us think that meaningful reality lies directly behind the signs once we have succeeded in deciphering them." This technique is a prevalent one in constructing the textuality for cosmetic products. For example, ads for perfume and cologne by Ralph Lauren, for Boucheron, DKNY, and Eternity (Calvin Klein), simply show the bottle alone as a work of sculpture art (the bottle itself), suggesting its idolatry, or else showcase couples in romantic embrace or models in various sexual poses with the bottle in the foreground or background.

Needless to say, this technique is rarely used in commercials, given that they are miniature dramas or skits. In this case, it is the tone of voice, the register (friendly, authoritative, etc.), and the use of various rhetorical devices (jingles, slogans, etc.) that are deployed commonly to create brand textuality. The tone of voice can be seductive, friendly, cheery, insistent, foreboding, etc. as required. The register is informal and colloquial for brands such as Budweiser, but formal and elegant for brands such as the BMW and Mercedes-Benz automobiles. Advertising borrows from discourse styles and various television and movie trends to suit its purposes. A commercial can take the form of an interview; a testimonial on the part of a celebrity; an official format (Name: Mary; Age: 15; Problem: acne), etc.

A sixth major technique, which may be called a "gossip" strategy, is based on the fact that gossip and secrets grab our attention: "Don't tell your friends about . . ."; "Do you know what she's wearing?" "Does she or doesn't she? Only her hairdresser knows for sure"; etc. To put it simply, gossip appeals. As British author Paul Scott (1920–78) aptly put it in his novel *The Day of the Scorpions* (University of Chicago Press, 1968: 28): "The truth is always one thing, but in a way it's the other thing, the gossip, that counts. It shows where people's hearts lie."

A seventh major technique is the use of humor. Through humorous slogans, jingles, and commercials, many brands attempt not only to convey a friendly and "folk" image of themselves, but also to tap into current comedic styles. With its condensed style, its trendy slang form, and its ephemerality, ad humor is thus reflective of broader trends within pop culture. This is why the Budweiser campaigns are always so funny. They are, in a phrase, *au courant*.

A perfect example is the 2005 TV commercial campaign by the feminine birth control product Alesse, which played on a type of wry humor associated with the TV series *Sex and the City* that pitted women against men with the product functioning as "code" for women's secret knowledge. This commercial started with several young women of various ethnic backgrounds using the phrase "I'm on Alesse." They all wore different styles of clothing and their personalities also seemed very different. Only those familiar with the code could relate to the phrase until the end, when a young male appears on screen yelling: "What's Alesse?" The male looked utterly confused as an "outsider," and significantly did not receive a response to his question, as the women just chuckled dismissively. The final frame of the commercial revealed a package of oral contraceptives, providing the visual key to the "code."

Alesse represents an example of gendered humor. Another example was the 2005 Tampax tampon campaign, which featured a scene in a coed upper school classroom where a girl passes a note to another classmate. The other student tries to pass something back to her but is caught by the male teacher and asked to bring it to him. She walks to the front and hands him a small object wrapped in yellow paper. The teacher admonishes her with: "Ms Maggie, I hope you have enough for everyone." She replies: "Enough for the girls." The teacher looks confused, as do the boys in the classroom. The girls, on the other hand, giggle and look at each other knowingly.

Co-opting humor styles and comedic formulas is part of the textuality of many brands, occupying a central place in contemporary brand imagery. Even brands that once used a different textuality are now jumping on the humor bandwagon. Recent cases in point are Dairy Queen's commercials of a baby trying to steal his father's Cheesecake Sundae and a man who starts fires after eating a Flamethrower Burger, and the Six Flags commercials featuring a bald old man in a tuxedo who drives his vintage bus into neighborhoods and tap dances joyfully to the catchy tune "We want to party" (all in 2005).

Needless to say, there are other types of language strategies used by brands to construct their textuality—e.g. the use of foreign words to convey connotations of exoticness and refinement, the use of word layouts and different fonts, etc.

VISUAL DEVICES

Visual images in advertising bring out signification systems powerfully. People can picture faces and images much more accurately and quickly than they can recall words. This is why cartoon characters, computer graphics, and other visual devices are used to create textuality for a product—mouthwash bottles dance across the screen; automobiles turn into animals; etc. In lifestyle advertising, conveying appropriate body image is the most important device. In ads for Calvin Klein products, for instance, the females have a soft, slim body form, and the males a slim, muscular and obviously virile one.

In general, ads and commercials for perfume, clothes, alcoholic drinks, and other lifestyle products use models with similar types of bodies. The eye contact that the female is perceived to make with the viewer in many of these ads is particularly forceful as a sexual signifier. The pupils are generally dilated, as the Toronto–Lugano team found by viewing 35 randomly chosen ads. This comes as no surprise since the female face is perceived as more sexually attractive when the pupils are dilated. In fact, in earlier times in Italy, extracts of the drug belladonna were used for its cosmetic effect, given that it produces extreme dilation of the pupils. This drug is now used by eye doctors to facilitate eye examinations, but its cosmetic applications explain the origin of its name, which in Italian means "beautiful woman."

The fashion magazine genre offers a perfect example of how visuality creates a powerful form of textuality, intertwining texts, colors, advertisements, and celebrity gossip. One such magazine, examined by the Toronto–Lugano team in 2003, is *In Style*, a popular women's fashion magazine, founded in 1994 by Martha Nelson and which currently publishes 13 issues annually (www.instyle.com/instyle/flash/0,24293, 1153050,00.html). Its circulation per issue is estimated at two-and-a-half million readers. Each *In Style* monthly issue is organized in a set pattern, to establish visual continuity between the brands it advertises, its articles and even its website. *In Style* thus creates a fashionably sophisticated textuality for its readers. Each edition of *In Style* features a pop-culture celebrity on the cover. The feature article is placed a few pages from the back of the issue, suggesting that the reader should peruse various fashion articles first. The typical *In Style* layout begins with an "Editor's Note," which synthesizes the articles found in that particular issue, followed by "The Look," which outlines current clothing trends among celebrities. This is followed by "Wardrobe Rx," which features a different popular item each month, providing the reader with advice on where to find some fashion item. The "I Want, I Need, I Have to Have

It" segment outlines one bargain buy, one good value buy, and one expensive item, which "every women should own." Information on where all three items can be purchased is also provided. Following are (respectively) the rubrics titled "Asset Management: Tips on Making the Most of Your Figure," "Ask Us," "Buy of the Month," "Instant Style," and "Fashion 101." The final sections are named "Beauty Talk," "Beauty Know-It-All," an article on the feature celebrity, a "Celebrity at-Home" feature, and a horoscope section. *In Style* rarely diverges from this format, as this layout, and the advertisements found throughout these articles, aid in generating the signification system that *In Style* wishes to create.

Each issue is replete with ads of perfumes, automobiles, credit cards, clothing, and other lifestyle products. A survey of ten random *In Style* issues published between 2001 and 2003 revealed that approximately 56 percent of magazine space was devoted to advertisements, and 44 percent to rubrics and articles. How does a women's magazine with such a high number of advertisements manage to generate such a large readership base? The answer lies arguably in the textuality of *In Style*. The advertisements, the rubrics, and the articles form a uniform text, as each ad visually illustrates the topics of the articles, generating a seamless continuity between the articles and the products being advertised. For example, in the September 2003 issue (pp. 267–70), the advertisements found throughout an article entitled "The Ultimate Shoe Guide" featured different varieties of shoes and purses.

These images are powerful in creating imaginary ideas of how a woman wants herself to appear, which aid in promoting consumer products (DeLong and Bye 1990; Mandoki 2003). *In Style* is itself a hypertext of products and lifestyle ideas, integrating texts of different kinds that are, nevertheless, based on similar or overlapping signification systems. It has been found that people easily identify with what they read and more importantly what they see in such magazines because they create the illusion of thematic unity (Hegglie 1993; Aronson 2000). Through its "integrated textual structure," *In Style* creates a signification system for itself that intertwines with the signification systems of its ad texts.

METATEXTUALITY

Ingenious ads, clever names, mythic logos, text layouts, and the like would have virtually no effect in ensconcing brand image if they "did not get out there," to put it figuratively. The survival of brands in today's marketplace depends largely on the use of different media to spread the word (the signification systems). This, in itself, creates a Just-So effect for the brands, producing the perception that they have a necessary role to play in society.

As mentioned in the opening chapter, information about the availability, quality, and price of goods and services was spread by word of mouth and poster signs in the ancient and medieval worlds. The information thus reached very few people. But this situation changed drastically with the invention of the movable-type printing press in Europe in the mid-fifteenth century.

The advent of print technology gave merchants the means to reach many more people through direct mail. As a consequence, it led to the rise of a whole new business—typography—that made possible the mass production of leaflets, brochures, catalogues, and other printed materials that could be delivered by a postal service or spread widely by other means. It also gave more importance to the outdoor sign-making business. Enhanced technology allowed merchants to print posters cheaply. In the nineteenth century, the large-scale industrialization of cities created a need for extensive advertising, leading to the invention of lithography, a printing method that made it easier to include colored illustrations on print materials. Beginning in 1867, the artist Jules Chéret revolutionized the look of posters, using illustrations as dominant features while reducing the verbal text to a minor explanatory role. Chéret's method gave rise to the practice of printing visually charming commercial posters that could appeal instantly to people (literate or not). His techniques continue to be used to this day. In the 1890s, several art nouveau artists introduced other important innovations in the craft of print advertising—namely, the use of large areas of flat color and the replacement of the idealized figures of human beings with naturalistic or caricatured figures depicted in telling vignettes. The art nouveau artists also introduced flowing lines and elegant, elongated forms to create exotic, stylized illustrations. Their techniques are also being used to this very day.

Using all kinds of media—print, electronic, and digital—the so-called "big brands" also employ a technique that can be called "metatextuality," defined simply as creating different kinds of texts for each medium creating an overall text, or "metatext" to promote their products. Metatextuality is established by ad campaigns, which constitute systematic methods of advertising brands that may run for several months, or more, through the use of different media. Ad campaigns are characterized, in fact, by a series of slightly different ad texts based on the same theme, characters, jingles, etc. An ad campaign is comparable to the theme-and-variations form of music, where there is one theme with many variations. But the variations (different texts) cohere into an over-arching text (theme) which, as mentioned, can be called a metatext.

Along with the other electronic media—radio and television—the internet has become a powerful source of brand diffusion. Each of these media requires commentary here. Radio broadcasting allowed brand imagery to be spread more widely than did newspapers and magazines in the early 1920s, reaching the pinnacle of its popularity and influence during World War II. The radio brought news, information, the arts, and (most significantly) brand advertising directly into homes. The parallel growth of network radio and Hollywood cinema, both of which were launched as commercial enterprises in the 1920s, created an unprecedented mass culture for people of all social classes and educational backgrounds. Only after the advent of television in the 1950s did radio's hegemony begin to erode, as its audiences split into smaller, distinct segments.

Like magazines, radio programs are integrated with brand advertising and are sponsored by brands of various kinds, positioned for specific audiences. The soap-opera genre was even named for the type of advertiser—soap companies—that sponsored them. In the US, advertising agencies produced almost all network radio shows before the development of network television. Stations often sold agencies full sponsorship, which included placing the product name in a program's title, as with Palmolive Beauty Box Theater (1927–37) or The Texaco Star Theatre (1948–53). Entire radio programs became associated with specific brands. The ratings system arose, in fact, from the sponsors' desire to know how many people they were reaching with their advertising. In 1929 Archibald Crossley launched Crossley's Cooperative Analysis of Broadcasting, using telephone surveys to project daily estimates of audience size for the national radio networks. The A. C. Nielsen Company, which had been surveying audience size in radio since the mid-1930s, eventually became the dominant ratings service. The ratings helped set the price of advertisements and, ultimately, whether the program would stay on the air or be canceled. Only public radio stations are exempt from the "ratings game," for the reason that they are financed by government subsidies, individual donations, and corporate grants.

Radio introduced the commercial into advertising—a mini-narrative or musical jingle revolving around a product or service and its uses. The commercial could reach masses of potential customers, print literate or not, instantaneously through the persuasive power of the human voice. Radio commercials of the day consisted of pseudoscientific sales pitches, satires of movies, and snappy jingles. They became so familiar that perception of the product became inextricably intertwined with the style and content of the commercials created to promote it. The commercial form also created the first brand personalities, such as Mr Clean and Speedy.

Since the advent of radio advertising, simple, repetitive, and catchy slogans and jingles, as mentioned above, have become an intrinsic part of the construction of brand textuality and a means of establishing meta-textuality for a brand. Here are some famous slogans and jingles (Karmen 1989):

- You deserve a break today, so get up and get up and get away. (McDonald's)
- I'm loving it. (McDonald's)
- Be all that you can be. (US Army)
- Pepsi-Cola hits the spot. (Pepsi-Cola)
- M'm, M'm, good. (Campbell's Soup)
- See the USA in Your Chevrolet. (General Motors)
- Double your pleasure, double your fun. (Wrigley's Doublemint Gum)
- It's the real thing. (Coca-Cola)
- A little dab'll do ya. (Brylcreem)

Sometimes, the brand engages a pop music icon and his or her song as its signature jingle. For example, David Bowie's "Rebel, rebel" has been used to pitch Audi cars, Cyndi Lauper's "Girls just wanna have fun" to promote Carnival Cruises, and Bob Seger's "Like a rock" to sell Chevy trucks. The jingle, like the name and logo, is a device that creates a culturally strategic image for a brand. Essentially, the jingle is a musical slogan—a memorable melody married perfectly to its lyrics. This synchronization of music with brand can be seen throughout contemporary advertising. For example, classic rock and roll is often used to accompany commercials of expensive automobiles. The classic example of this is General Motors' adoption of Led Zeppelin's 1971 anthem "Rock and roll" for its Cadillac campaign in the early 2000s.

The radio medium is still pivotal as a means to establish brand popularity through jingles. A synergy continues to exist between radio advertising campaigns and musical trends. Radio advertising has the advantage that people can listen to programs while doing other things, such as driving a car or working at home. Another advantage is that radio audiences, in general, are more highly selectable by program genre than are television audiences. For example, stations that feature country music attract different kinds of listeners than do those that play rock.

Since the mid-1950s, television has become a very powerful medium for delivering brand image, bringing sight, sound, and action directly to consumers in their homes. The majority of TV commercials consist of short spot announcements, most of which last 30 seconds to a minute. The commercials are usually run in groups of three to six or nine. Television networks and stations generally limit commercial time to about 10 minutes per hour during prime time and 16 minutes per hour during most other broadcast times. TV is a major player in the creation of brand metatextuality. The same kinds of ad texts and devices used for radio are adapted to the TV medium.

Today, satellite television and the internet have joined forces, so to speak, to make it possible for brands to spread the word about themselves all over the globe, regardless of time zone or political boundary. This is why the commercial use of the internet has grown dramatically since the mid-1990s. Virtually any product or service can now be ordered from internet sites. In 2002 the Nielsen/Net Ratings firm counted nearly 70,000 commercials on the internet during the single month of May.

It is little wonder that the major brands have taken to the Web with great enthusiasm. For example, in 2001 the carmaker BMW hired several famous directors to make short "digital films" featuring its cars. The movies were viewable only on the Web, but were also promoted through TV spots. Those digital commercials clearly blurred the line between art and advertising, showing how a continuity had emerged between the larger cultural order and brand-based textuality. Each film was about 6 minutes long; each featured a prominent actor; and each portrayed BMWs used in a reckless, adventure-oriented fashion.

The blurring of lines between long-standing representational activities (artistic, linguistic, etc.) within the larger cultural order and those generated by brands can be called, simply, "convergence," a course of action designed to create a sense of continuity between the products advertised and the various artistic and social activities of the culture. Convergence can be seen both across media and within a specific medium. The former can be seen clearly in ad campaigns for high-tech products, such as iPods, cellphones, digital cameras, and Palm Pilots, which are constantly related to youth lifestyles in all kinds of magazine and electronic media. These have gone from being useful new devices to fashion trends, becoming part of the fashion gear carried by adolescents in many parts of the modern world. They have, in effect, created their own kind of metatextuality. The convergence of product advertising with magazine contents is an example of convergence within a specific medium. This is found not only in specialized magazines, as we saw above, but also in those that advertise different types of products:

- Chanel products, for instance, are related to the interests of female audiences who read magazines such as *Vogue*.
- Nike shoes are related to the interests of trendy adolescent and young adult audiences who read magazines such as *Seventeen*.
- Audis and BMWs are related to the interests of an up-scale class of automobile customers who read magazines such as *Esquire*.
- Dodge vans are related to the interests of a middle-class suburban consumer population who read magazines such as *Look*.

As we saw above with *In Style* magazine, there are myriads of similar magazines where convergence brand signification systems and magazine contents inform the structure of the magazine. Throughout women's magazines such as *Vogue* and *Glamour* one can see images of models wearing designer clothes and cosmetics interspersed with articles about fashion and physical appearance. As Dyer noted some time ago, this blurring of brand textuality with other kinds of textualities creates

> structures of meaning which sell commodities not for themselves as useful objects but in terms of ourselves as social beings in our different social relationships. Products are given 'exchange-value': ads translate statements about objects into statements about types of consumer and human relationships.
>
> (1982: 116)

In sum, multi-media and convergent styles of advertising have extended the reach of brands into virtually all domains of society. Ads appear in movie theaters and on DVDs prior to the featured movie. They appear on ski-lift towers, and in high-school classroom news programming. In supermarkets, shoppers may be exposed to in-store radio, grocery carts with miniature billboards or video screens, and TV sets with programs or commercials in the checkout line. In fact, it is no exaggeration to say that vast portions of cultural space—physical and mental—have become branded. No wonder, then, that the same techniques used by manufacturers are now used by virtually anyone seeking to gain attention within that space. Already in 1952, politics got into the "advertising game," when Dwight D. Eisenhower successfully ran for the US presidency, with the help of advertising executives, who directed Eisenhower's presidential campaign. Since then, advertising has played an increasingly important role in political campaigns, with TV spot announcements having become a major strategy of campaigns for public offices at all levels of government. "It pays to advertise," has become the salient aphorism of the contemporary world.

If the textuality of brands has become co-extensive with that of other textualities, then, one far-reaching feature of contemporary life should be considered as hardly surprising: the branding of culture. The next chapter considers arguments about this phenomenon and analyzes the branding strategies that have become dispersed across a great part of social life in industrialized society.

5

THE BRANDING
OF CULTURE

We live in a world ruled by fictions of every kind—mass merchandising, advertising, politics conducted as a branch of advertising, the instant translation of science and technology into popular imagery, the increasing blurring and intermingling of identities within the realm of consumer goods, the preempting of any free or original imaginative response to experience by the television screen. We live inside an enormous novel. For the writer in particular it is less and less necessary for him to invent the fictional content of his novel. The fiction is already there. The writer's task is to invent the reality.

J. G. Ballard (1930–)

Brands are now everywhere, having become integral components in the constitution of modern-day consumerist cultures. The branding of culture is the focus of this chapter. Specifically, I will look at how brands attempt to build and solidify a semiotic bridge between the product, media, and cultural performances.

The term "branding" is used in the relevant cultural studies literature to refer to the process whereby the messages of brand advertising and those of other cultural sectors are no longer perceived as different. Companies no longer aim their ad campaigns at appropriate market segments; rather, they make them reflect general trends (recreational, artistic, etc.) within the larger culture. Moreover, they aim to become themselves "part of the entertainment scene," so to say, in various ways. Revlon, for instance, spent millions of dollars in the early 2000s for close-up shots of its product during the broadcasting of the American TV soap opera, *All My Children*. And this is a branding exercise that is only taking place within the bounds of a fictional television programme. There are many brands that also enthusiastically sponsor socially significant events in the real world, from demonstrations against poverty to sporting spectacles.

BRANDING STRATEGIES

The integration of brand image with pop culture has, actually, always been the implicit strategy in big brand marketing. As we saw in the previous chapter, major brands and the media formed a partnership early in the twentieth century. The "content" of the entertainment-artistic world has since become increasingly more "branded." Brands are now being showcased in one form or other in movies, TV programs, and other cultural domains. "Brand placement," as it is called, has become the most effective (in terms of reaching consumers) of all the branding strategies ever devised.

In the 1950s brand placement was a simple matter. In TV programs such as Texaco Theater, General Electric Theater and Kraft Theater, the television program itself was associated exclusively with one sponsor. Children's programming, such as *Mickey Mouse Club* (which premiered in 1955), was similarly sponsored. The show used young actors hired by Disney who became themselves icons of child culture, promoting the whole Disney brand of products (from movies to dolls). But this form of sponsorship was not applicable to all kinds of programs and formats. In its lieu, other placing strategies soon crystallized and spread across the media. Often, the sponsor would be included as part of the script, thus making the distinction between program content and sponsor a blurry one. The movies entered the placement fray in 1982 when the extra-terrestrial creature in Stephen Spielberg's ET was seen snacking on Reese's Pieces—increasing sales for the product enormously. That event started a trend in Hollywood. In 1983, for example, movie actor Tom Cruise donned a pair of Wayfarers (Ray-Ban sunglasses) in *Risky Business*, and sales for the product shot up, as did generally the wearing of similar sunglasses to convey a "cool look" (for it should be remembered that brand placement can also promote fake or cheaper versions of the main brand being promoted).

The placement of brands in the scripts of TV programs and movies is now so common that the strategy itself goes largely unnoticed. Its main objective is to amalgamate brand identity with pop-culture textualities. A good example of this amalgamation was the launch of the teenage-targeted television serial *Dawson's Creek* in January 1998. All the characters in the program were outfitted in clothing and accessories made by J. Crew. They appeared, in fact, to be models that had stepped out of the J. Crew catalogue, and the actors were featured in that catalogue the very same month. Two seasons later, as the "cool look" changed in society, the characters received a makeover and new wardrobe from American Eagle Outfitters. And, once again, the company used the actors as models for their own purposes, featuring them on their website and in-store promotions.

The main marketing strategy adopted by brands today is one that links products to actors, music celebrities, and the like, obfuscating product promotion, entertainment, and lifestyle patterns. Celebrity endorsement of a brand is now commonplace. It is an effective strategy because it transfers what people perceive in the celebrity to the product. So, too, is the creation of new fictitious characters to promote specific brands. Many of these have become cultural celebrities themselves, independently of the products they represent. In America, Mr Clean, Uncle Ben, Charlie the Tuna, and Hostess' Twinkie the Kid have become such an intrinsic part of cultural lore that they were even featured in cameo roles in a 2001 animated film called *Foodfight*. And in the same year, Barbie became a ballerina in the movie *Barbie in the Nutcracker*.

Sometimes, the product itself becomes a fad, dictating and creating larger trends in society. In the 1950s, Silly Putty, Slinkies, and Hula Hoops became so popular that they were the inspiration of songs and narratives. Silly Putty was introduced in 1949 by advertising marketer Peter C. L. Hodgson, who discovered a substance developed by General Electric researchers looking for a viable synthetic rubber. The useless silicone substance could be molded like soft clay, stretched like taffy, and bounced like a rubber ball. Slinky was a coil toy that could be made to "walk" down a staircase by itself by placing it on a higher step in a specific way. The Hula Hoop was a light plastic hoop that could be whirled around the body for play or exercise by the movement of the hips. These products became icons of pop culture, remaining so to this day, because they were promoted constantly through the media. As such products became a craze, the brand need not be promoted directly by advertising, marketing, or other such "above-the-line" activities. Instead, the product, especially when branded, could be the focus of television coverage of the craze, thus placing it within a "below-the-line" strategy. Brand placement is, in a way, somewhere between direct, above-the-line marketing (as with the example of Revlon, it is paid for) and promotional, below-the-line marketing (it does not seem to be straightforward advertising, but merely part of the fabric of what the medium is presenting in general).

With new media, placement and other forms of branding are becoming easier and easier to realize. The toymaker Mattel, for instance, has a Planet Hot Wheels website from which one can download a game or play one online. Hot Wheels are small toy cars made to resemble real cars. They are cheap and highly popular with young boys. The website is intended to impart a "cool image" to the brand so as to attract teenagers and so-called tweenies (prepubescent children) to whom little children look up. The site offers upgrades for "virtual vehicles" and a motocross 1950s' drag-race game, which are free with a Hot Wheels purchase. The image that Mattel is trying to promote is one that can be encapsulated by the following signification system: Hot Wheels = cool lifestyle = power, speed, performance = youth = etc. In early 2002, Mattel started supplying the toy cars to retailers such as AutoZone, frequented by the fathers of the children and the teens, thus extending its connotative reach intergenerationally.

The Mattel case is actually part of a spreading new form of branding, which can be called "embedding." Embedding can involve co-operation among brands. The site, neopet.com, is a case in point. Offering a host of recreational and educational activities to children, in 2004 it created a virtual McDonald's site, a Lucky Charms game, and other brand embeds in it. Below are three other examples of brand embedding:

- In 2001, the Prada Company embedded itself in some stores by installing a high-tech system in them that allowed customers to request sizes and colors for garments by touching a computer screen.
- In 2002, Listerine provided a matching key chain with its PocketPaks, which was given away at the 2002 Oscars, at the Golden Globes, and at modeling agencies.
- Wrigley's Winterfresh was distributed at the 2002 MTV Music Awards and at the Extreme Games of that year, blurring the distinction between the events and the product.

Another form of branding can be called "brand co-optioning." For example, the Pillsbury Doughboy was co-opted by the Sprint Corporation in 2004 and 2005 to promote their product in a campaign in which he paired up with the Sprint Guy. Similarly, the Maytag repairman turned up in an ad for the Chevrolet Impala and the Taco Bell Chihuahua appeared in an ad for Geico. This indicates psychologically that consumers obviously develop a relationship with the specific brands they love and that this can be used to promote other brands.

"Co-branding," as it is called, can also be seen to constitute a type of brand co-option. For example, the co-branding of various bookstore chains with coffee giants such as *Starbucks* involves combining the connotations of intellectualism (symbolized by books) with coffee consumption, and the two share a long history of connected meanings. The "Paris coffee scene," as it can be called, evokes images of intellectuals discussing their ideas while sipping coffee in a café in Paris. Furthermore, Jurgen Habermas's (1989) influential thesis on the growth of a public sphere of rational debate is precisely associated with the massive growth in coffee shops in Europe from the early eighteenth century onwards. With the serving of a "brand coffee" in a bookstore, the same kind of scene is evoked in an imaginary way. Sipping coffee in the intellectual atmosphere associated with a bookstore reverberates with "Paris café" connotations, conjuring up images of intellectuals discussing life, art, culture, science, and the like at chic cafés. This "blended signification system" is actually in line with the history of coffee itself, which was originally viewed as an exotic substance. Co-branding constitutes, as this case in point brings out, a kind of "semiotic chemical mixture," whereby the connotative meanings of two signification systems fuse into a new one.

The subtext of co-branding implicates the image of individuals who enjoy the finer things in life, and who are cultured in a well-rounded way. Actually, the association of brands with intellectualism and the arts is a long-standing one. Those with political, religious, or economic power have always attempted to promote themselves as cultured by becoming patrons of the arts. Sponsoring arts events is a way to gain respect, authority, and to reveal concern for the culture in which a sponsor exists. In the past, artists (such as classical music composers) would dedicate their works to a benefactor or sponsor, acknowledging the benefactor's help and support. Strangely, this has not yet occurred when the sponsor is a brand. To the best of my knowledge, while there have been name-checks for various brands (e.g. the tobacco "Ogden's Nut Gone Flake," the name of the classic Small Faces album of 1967), there has never been a case of an artist actually *dedicating* something to a cigarette brand, a beer manufacturer, or the like.

Another way that brands blur the lines between themselves and the general culture is by creating ads and commercials that are, simply, enjoyable to masses of people in and of themselves. As we saw in the previous chapter, some ads have become so ingenious that they are no longer distinguishable from art works. A 2002 *USA Today* survey of the most popular TV commercials that were being aired at the time revealed that they were among the most popular texts in the city of Toronto by the research team (Table 5.1). Of the 45 people interviewed in that city,

Table 5.1 Popular 2002 commercials

Company	Description of commercial
1 Anheuser-Busch	A romantic evening goes awry with satin sheets
2 Anheuser-Busch	A pet falcon hunts bottles of Bud Light
3 Anheuser-Busch	Cedric the entertainer plays matchmaker
4 Anheuser-Busch	A bunch of "Jersey guys" encounter a big-mouthed Texan
5 Anheuser-Busch	A minifridge fights BattleBot for a bottle of Bud Light
6 Blockbuster Video	Pets dance after watching people rent videos
7 Charles Schwab	Baseball legend Hank Aaron advises the new legend Barry Bonds to retire
8 E-Trade	A monkey is showcased in a musical
9 Levi's	A young man crossing a street finds his legs "have the moves"
10 Lipton Brisk	Danny De Vito begins a revolt after some puppets are fired

virtually everyone claimed to enjoy the commercials in the same way that they enjoyed TV sitcoms, or even more so.

Some brands attempt to blur the lines by showing themselves to be involved in, or sensitive to, social issues. For example, Natural American Spirit Cigarettes (Santa Fe Natural Tobacco Co.) put the following "politically correct" acknowledgment on its packages in the early 2000s: "We make no representation, either expressed or implied, that these cigarettes are any less hazardous than any other cigarettes." This was a transparent ploy to convey an image of itself as an environmentally concerned and socially responsible brand. Indeed, it almost seems to negate the act of branding, admitting the negative aspects of smoking. The cigarette packs also contained fliers featuring endangered species, and supporting statements of small-scale farmers.

Elsewhere, a brand might make itself seem socially committed in a more subtle way, without overt statements. In the early 1990s, Levi's advertised their jeans on television and the cinema using the Clash song "Should I stay or should I go?" (from the 1982 *Combat Rock* album). For some consumers, the music simply represented a catchy rock and roll song appropriate to Levi's image. To those who know anything about the Clash and their political commitments, especially those espoused on *Combat Rock*, it was clear that Levi's was attempting to co-opt hip radicalism.

In sum, the most successful brands are those that have become part of cultural meaning systems. No wonder, then, that advertisers, marketers, and the brand manufacturers themselves are employing academic experts from the fields of psychology, anthropology, linguistics, communications, media studies, culture studies, and semiotics on an increasingly regular basis. On the one hand, this too is arguably a ploy to appear authoritative before clients; on the other hand, it is a sure sign that there is a growing "academic culture" within the marketing world itself that is starting to produce its own forms of legitimization—academically styled reports, journals, websites, and a body of research literature. This imparts an aura of "scientificity" to the whole branding business itself, allowing it even more so to become an integral part of the social landscape. Journals such as the *DMI Journal,* the *Journal of Brand Management*, the *International Journal of Research in Marketing*, and the *Journal of Advertising*, to mention a few, contain case studies in branding, logo design, package design, etc. that allow for the documentation and establishment of a research database on brands.

The number of companies and websites offering expert advice for branding has reached mind-boggling proportions. Using several search engines, I counted over 100,000 distinct websites in early 2005 concerned with offering advice on how to create a brand image or how an established brand can rejuvenate or revitalize its image. The names of these companies are revealing in themselves, since they emphasize how critical the process of constructing brand image has become. Here are a few company names, chosen at random, that are self-explanatory:

–   Brand Fidelity
–   Brand Institute
–   Catchword
–   Connotion ("connotation" + "notion")
–   Metaphor Name Consultants
–   NameLab
–   Namestormers ("names" + "brainstormers")
–   Namewise
–   Naming Systems
–   Namix
–   Strategic Name Development

The number of such companies and sites that now explicitly use, or profess to use, semiotics is also significant. I counted nearly 1,000 such sites, indicating a growing awareness of the power of semiotics to frame the relevant issues in brand image and branding. Some sites overtly flaunt their association with semiotics. There are also magazines (paper-based and online) that specialize in brand-based research. Magazines such as *Meredith Integrated Marketing*, *BrandPackaging*, and *Brandquiver.com* now present data, case studies, and the like on branding experiences.

It would appear that the century-old goal of brands to become integral parts of the cultural landscape may have finally been achieved. The problem now is hardly just the matter of acceptance by the cultural mainstream, but rather how to maintain an edge in it through constant innovation. This is particularly crucial when the perceptions of a product change. As discussed in the previous two chapters, the establishment of brand identity occurs the instant a product is assigned a name. However, if the identity becomes tarnished, then a change is required. This explains the decision by the Phillip Morris Company to change its name to Altria Group (from Latin *altus* "high" + *altrui*, "other, altruism"), so as to establish a new image of the company by word association. The previous association with tobacco products was obviously doing damage to its image ever since 1996, when legislation placing sharp restrictions on cigarette advertising was passed by the US Congress to keep Joe Camel and the Marlboro Man away from children. Philip Morris and other companies mounted legal challenges to the restrictions, but the damage to their image was done. Changing its name to suggest that the company does indeed care about people is the obvious rationale behind the change.

The newer generations of consumers are warier of the branding ploys than were their parents and grandparents, given that they have been exposed to mass marketing since birth. The marketing savvy of consumers today makes them shy away from campaigns that tell them that their lives will be changed by adopting a certain brand. This is why brands such as Smirnoff Vodka now promote their products by entreating people "to join the party," implying that they would otherwise be marginalized socially. Honda, too, inveigles consumers to join the in-crowd by becoming a member of Honda's "Civic Nation," with its hip-hop music commercials and images of street racing. Apple, too, warns young consumers that without possessing an iPod they might be left, by implication, out of the "night club scene" where the iPod itself brings people together in a bacchanalia of fun and friendship, suffused with the promise of sexual activities.

As Douglas Atkin (2004) argues, brands strive to develop a cult-like effect on people, endeavoring to turn them into devotees in ways that are not unlike those utilized by real cults. As he observes, the salient characteristic of the recent approach by brands such as Smirnoff and

Apple is that they promise to unite people through a shared experience and trust—the exact same promise that attracts people to religions and cults. Consumption has clearly replaced religion as an experience of life. Cult brands such as the iPod seem to answer the need for gregariousness by creating virtual and real communities. Providing the comfort of real communities are brands such as Mary Kay cosmetics, Saturn automobiles, and Snapple beverages, aided by clever campaigns that emphasize that users of the brands form a specific type of community.

Ironically, trends in pop culture generated by branding strategies are now co-opted by religions themselves. The fitness craze in pop culture is a case in point. Influenced no doubt by evangelical images of bodily ideals as featured, for instance, in the massively successful *Left Behind* series co-written by two evangelicals, Tim LaHaye and Jerry B. Jenkins, fundamentalist Christian groups in the US now equate lean and muscular bodies with spirituality—an association exploited by Mel Gibson in his 2004 blockbuster movie *The Passion of the Christ*, in which the character who played Christ looked muscular and virile, even while he was being crucified. The meanings of this kind of body image hark back to the muscular Christianity of the Crusades, when men in particular were expected to be robust and women highly disciplined. On the one hand, obesity suggests weakness, indulgence, lack of discipline, laziness, and all the egregious sins that these entail. On the other hand, Crusaders were supposed to be ready to die for their cause. The religious idealization of the body is certainly not an invention of modern-day American evangelicals. But its equation with dieting fads is. The Christian "food restraint movement" has adopted the same kind of slender beauty ideals of the secular culture. Both, ironically, contrast with attitudes throughout much of the developing and impoverished world that have long associated the fuller figure with beauty, wealth, merit, and divine blessing. In the context of world hunger, it might be argued that the branding of the slim body by the secular and evangelical worlds borders on the obscene.

The co-option of pop-culture trends by the very religious people who condemn them does not stop at dieting. As Possamai (2005) has discussed, fundamentalists claim to resist pop culture, but nevertheless appropriate it to promote their own religious views—e.g. Christian super-hero comics, role-playing games, Bible-based PC games, and "White Metal" music. The irony is unmistakable. The very ones who condemn the branding of culture are using the same kinds of techniques to brand themselves into the cultural mainstream.

Figure 5.1 A 2004 Guinness ad based on an evolution theme

WORD ASSOCIATION GAMES

A 2004 Guinness ad campaign constitutes a truly interesting example of the current state of affairs in the area of branding. Its implicit message is that brands evolve in the same way that organisms and species do (Figure 5.1).

The ad shows in simplistic form the evolution of "man," from *Australopithecus* to *Homo sapiens* (modern man). The next stage of evolution is "Guinness," a stage that will finally transform humanity into a species possessing "pure genius." Although the ad constitutes an exemplar of "absurdist humor," it also contains a clear subtext—the modern evolution of humans is the same as the evolution of humanity's greatest achievement—the brand! In textual terms, it constitutes an interesting example of a word association game (WAG)—a strategy that is a central one in modern-day branding efforts and is particularly pertinent to the drawing together of brands and general culture.

As discussed in previous chapters, naming a product creates a connotative signification system—a system that is by its very nature associative. For example, recall the type of WAGs that automobile manufacturers deploy in naming their cars.

As Table 5.2 shows, WAGs allow the carmakers to link automobiles with aspects of psychological and social life. Here are a few others:

- upscaleness (Park Avenue, Fifth Avenue, Catalina, Monte Carlo, Capri, etc.);
- social rank (Viscount, Marquis, Diplomat, Monarch, Ambassador, etc.);
- animal personality characteristics (Viper, Mustang, Cobra, etc.);
- open geographic terrain (Dakota, Montana, Yukon, Sierra, etc.).

Table 5.2 Word association games in automobile names

Name	Suggests that . . .
Aries, Taurus, etc.	an individual can drive a car that is compatible with his/her zodiac sign
Aspire	the vehicle allows one to realize one's ambitions
Breeze	the driver will feel a breeze by driving the vehicle and that driving the vehicle is "a breeze," i.e. something easy to do
Caravan	the vehicle is associated with gypsy life and, hence, with freedom and free-spiritedness
Cougar	the driver can morph into a cougar
Eclipse	driving the vehicle allows one to outshine or overshadow others
Excel	the vehicle allows its driver to go beyond a limit or standard, to perform at a level higher than that of another
Intrigue	something intriguing can be gained by driving the automobile
Mystique	the car is endowed with a special mystique and charisma
Neon	the vehicle gives the driver access to city life (with its "neon lights")
Odyssey	the vehicle will allow the driver to go on an odyssey—an adventurous voyage or a spiritual quest
Pathfinder	the vehicle will allow its driver to discover a new course or way into unexplored regions
Solara	driving the vehicle allows one to escape to the countryside where the "sun always shines"

Without such WAGs, the chance of brand failure increases considerably. A few of the great naming failures in the history of brands can be recalled here by way of illustration. In the 1950s, the Edsel car make, named after one of Henry Ford's sons, was a total failure (Atwan 1979). Although the look of the automobile is often cited as one of the reasons for this failure, there is little doubt in my mind that its name was a significant factor as well, since it could not be associated with anything recognizable in people's imaginations. Ford's 1988 Probe, which was targeted to young female first-time buyers, was another dismal economic failure, given the phallic connotations of its name; and Chevrolet's Nova failure is now seen as a classic case of unwitting associationism—the name-givers had not taken account of the fact that "no va" means "no go" in Spanish, leading to a disastrous sales record in Hispanic markets.

Table 5.3 Car names by Toyota illustrating the use of word association

Name	Connotations/associations
Avalon	The name is taken from Arthurian legend. Avalon is the mystical and earthly paradise to which King Arthur was led to receive his legendary sword.
Camry	The word sounds like the Japanese word for "small crown."
Corolla	The name comes from the term for the inside petals of a flower (which make up the "genitalia" of plants).
4Runner	The name combines "four-wheel drive off-road runner" and the word "forerunner," meaning pioneer or trendsetter.
Lexus	This coined name suggests "luxury" and classicism (since it emulates the form of a Latin noun).
Paseo	The name is Spanish for "pleasant trip."
Rav4	"Recreational active vehicle with four-wheel drive."
Sienna	The name has no specific meaning, but it suggests serenity or peacefulness through its sound symbolism (implying that parents are the targeted consumer). It also evokes an image of the color of burnt sienna, which produces a pleasant effect on the eye.
Supra	The name is a variation of "super" or "supreme."
Tacoma	The name is a Native American word for Mount Ranier, meaning "the place from whence the waters came." It is also the name of a city in Washington State, near Seattle, which also evokes images of the outdoors.
Tercel	The name is a variation of "tiercel," a male hawk known for its compact size.
T100	The name refers to the Toyota Truck 100 Series, where 100 designates "intermediate" capabilities.

Of all the automobile companies, Toyota has shown a remarkable ability to play WAGs better than most other carmakers. Table 5.3 lists some examples.

Toyota's XR Matrix and Scion xA require special mention since, to my mind, they are examples of truly ingenious WAGs. Both cars are intended to appeal to young, "multitasking" professionals who have embraced all kinds of digital technologies as a way of life and as a means to distinguish themselves from the authority structures of the business world of the past. The first name alludes as well to the 1999 hit movie of the same name starring Keanu Reeves. That movie has since become a cult classic among many young adults. It connotes sunglasses, shiny black leather jackets, digitized worlds, stylistic cool—a signification system that Toyota has obviously attempted to build into the brand name, which also includes the ubiquitous "X" factor discussed in Chapter 3. The Scion A name evokes a similar array of connotations—the word "scion" means a "descendant" and both the letters x (lower-case) and A (upper case) reverberate with meanings. Some of these have been discussed previously with regard to X. As for A, it is the first letter of the alphabet and thus "the first in a series," and "the best or highest in quality or rank." This blending of alphabetic symbolism with a noun is a new, powerful WAG trend, creating a sense of timelessness and excitement since it makes consumers discover something new and unheard of before.

The foregoing discussion is intended to emphasize that the youth market is a critical one for car manufacturers. For this reason, brand-naming practices have been adapted to trends and patterns within that market. WAGs are in synch with designs that make special sense to the constituents of that market segment. Table 5.4 lists three cases in point.

Similarly, WAGs are used by other types of products, indicating that the youth market is becoming increasingly dominant in world consumerism. Statistics show that video games continue to be highly popular among men in their twenties, thirties, and forties. For this reason, the names intended for youngsters in the 1970s and 1980s (when video games came onto the social scene)—PacMan, Pitfall, Pong, etc.—have been replaced with new, trendy names, such as those shown in Table 5.5.

Examples such as these abound in all areas of the contemporary marketplace. I will mention a few more examples for the sake of illustration. Heinz, for instance, started promoting its new Funky Fries line

Table 5.4 Relation established between automobile name and its design

Name	Design features
Acura's RDX	The car features seats that fold to make room for bikes; its name imitates the kind of alphabetic name given to bicycles
Dodge Razor	This car is an affordable stripped-down two-seater which, like a razor, is "sharp" and thus designed, by implication, for those just out of puberty
Mitsubishi's Saddle Bag	This car features doors that double as carrying cases, like saddle bags, a feature that is in synch with the fashion of carrying tote bags by young people

Table 5.5 Word association in game products

Name	Suggested meanings, associations, etc.
GameCub PlayStation	Rubik's Cube, video game parlors, contrast with "Work station" etc. (= intelligence, technology, etc.)
Gran Turismo	Gran Prix (= speed, power, coolness, etc.)
Grand Theft Auto Agent Under Fire	US, intrigue, life on the margins, excitement, cool, James Bond, etc.
Melee Metal Gear Solid	Car racing, adolescent-type clashes, free-for-alls (the 1987 film, *Full Metal Jacket*) etc.
Xbox Final Fantasy X	X-Files, X-rated movies, etc. (= forbidden pleasures, intrigue, mystery, etc.)

of fries in 2002 with new colors and shapes (Kool Blue, Crunchy Rings, Cocoa Crispers, Cinna-Sticks), so as to appeal to the "kiddy market." Brawny paper towels, to cite another case in point, once had a smiling blond-haired brawny lumberjack as its logo. The man looked like a 1970s porn star, so the company recently replaced him with a new Brawny man who looks like a contemporary car-racer (who has been emblazoned on car hoods that appeared in Nascar races). The idea for the change was to "modernize" the lumberjack look, while at the same time retaining its fundamental "macho" image. It is relevant to note that the previous Brawny man had become a kind of cultural icon—to wit: on an episode of the *Simpsons*, Marge Simpson became infatuated with the "Burly" paper-towel man (in obvious allusion to the Brawny man), kissing his picture on the package and writing him a fan letter. As one final example, a few years ago Old Spice changed its image to appeal to younger consumers with two new types of deodorant—a gel stick antiperspirant and an aerosol can. In 2002, a TV commercial for the product showed a guy cheating on his girlfriend, helped by his new Old Spice wipe, which erases one woman's kiss before he meets the next. Another commercial showed three guys coming out from a car after a long road-trip. Looking scruffy and bedraggled, they pass around the Cool Contact wipes. Suddenly, they are transformed into swank, debonair men in retro leather jackets and shades. The final scene of the commercial shows them swaggering into a Las Vegas casino, to the admiring stares of gorgeous-looking females.

One may ask why WAGs seem to work so effectively. Let me suggest that they work because society is willing to embrace consumerism with its implicit promise of pleasure for the masses. Mass culture is a revolutionary force, breaking down the old barriers of class, tradition, taste, and dissolving virtually all previous social distinctions. Kitsch is its aesthetic code. Consumption, therefore allows—at least psychologically, if only partially—the transcendence of such barriers and movement from one (consuming) identity to another. Such a movement is supposedly open to everybody, provided they have the necessary spending power. WAGs succeed because they encapsulate this promise.

AD CAMPAIGNS

Another key strategy the brands deploy to integrate themselves to the larger cultural order is, as discussed briefly in the previous chapter, the creation of metatextuality for themselves through ad campaigns. Already in 1892, the Coca-Cola Company spread its logo across the US, painting it as a mural on walls, displaying it on posters and soda fountains where the drink was served, and imprinting it on widely marketed, common household items (calendars, drinking glasses, etc.). Coca-Cola put out its first newspaper ad on May 29, 1886. In 1904, the Campbell's Soup Company mounted one of the first truly successful modern advertising campaigns featuring the rosy-cheeked Campbell Kids and the slogan "M'm! M'm Good!" Since then, all the big brands have used the ad campaign approach consistently and generally with great success.

One of the more successful types of ad campaign methods is the co-option of celebrities. In 1985, for instance, Nike signed basketball player Michael Jordan as its spokesperson, marking the beginning of a dramatic growth for the company. Nike then marketed the Air Jordan line of basketball shoes and clothes with a series of striking advertising creations which, along with the company's "Just Do It" slogan and campaign, featuring football and baseball star Bo Jackson and motion-picture director Spike Lee, boosted profits considerably. In 1997, Nike entered a new period of high-profile product image when the company hired Tiger Woods as its spokesperson. Woods was the first African and Asian American to win the Professional Golf Association's Masters golfing tournament.

Campaigns can have a profound impact on people. This is why they are now watched closely by lawmakers. In 1991, for example, the American Medical Association criticized RJR Nabisco for using a cartoon character named Joe Camel in its advertising campaigns, claiming that the company was targeting children. The Joe Camel ads conveyed a "cool image." The ads showed a camel, dressed in a "night clubbish" white jacket, smoking a cigarette dangling suggestively from the side of his mouth; the camel could be seen to "make eyes" at someone flirtatiously.

The camel conveyed the socialite smoothness and finesse represented by Thirties' and Forties' cinema stars, especially Humphrey Bogart in *Casablanca*. One year later, the US Surgeon General asked the company to withdraw its Joe Camel ads, and this request was followed by more government appeals in 1993 and 1994. The company responded to public concerns by promoting a campaign that encouraged store merchants and customers to obey the law prohibiting the sale of tobacco products to minors. In 1997, under increasing criticism, the company ended its Joe Camel ad campaign.

The brand appeared finally to be sensitive to social trends, and this perception no doubt played a role in increasing its profits in that very year. Campaigns by other brands quickly jumped on the bandwagon, utilizing, strategically, "anti-advertising" themes that were crystallizing in society at large. In 1997, for instance, a Nike campaign used the slogan "I am not a target, I am an athlete"; and Sprite used "Image is nothing."

Of all the brands, perhaps no one more than Pepsi has been successful at keeping in synch with the times, always emphasizing the changing social climate in its campaigns. The Pepsi product was invented in 1898 by an American pharmacist, named Caleb Bradham, who gave it the brand name Pepsi-Cola to highlight the fact that the pepsin in it was a digestive product. In 1903, Bradham produced the first ads for the product; these announced its pharmacological function simply as: "Exhilarating, Invigorating, Aids Digestion." To boost sales, however, in 1906, Pepsi started changing its image with the slogan "The Original Pure Food Drink," emphasizing the fact that the drink was not a chemical concoction, but a "pure" substance.

As society became more affluent, Pepsi changed its campaign in 1920 to "Drink Pepsi-Cola: It Will Satisfy You." But the Depression years forced Pepsi to change it in 1939 to "Twice as Much for a Nickel"—a Depression-sensitive theme introduced cleverly by the cartoon characters Peter and Pete. Pepsi had also become aware of the growing persuasive power of music on the radio. So in 1940, it became one of the first advertisers in history to broadcast a jingle called "Nickel, Nickel." It was so popular that it became a hit on its own. Throughout the 1940s, the Pepsi Company started tapping into the American Dream of "bigger and better," with campaigns such as "Bigger Drink, Better Taste" (1943) and "Why Take Less When Pepsi's Best?" (1949).

In the decade of the 1950s, Pepsi was among the first companies to start explicitly blending in with the youth culture trends that were taking hold of society. In 1950, with its "More Bounce to the Ounce" campaign, it emphasized the vigorous lifestyle that was in vogue in that era. In 1953–4, with a growing concern over obesity, Pepsi assumed a new weight-conscious personality with its campaign "The Light Refreshment and Refreshing without Filling." As pop culture became more and more youth-oriented in the late 1950s and 1960s, Pepsi followed suit. In 1958, Pepsi targeted the new teen market with "Be Sociable, Have a Pepsi."

Aware of the socioeconomic clout of adolescents, Pepsi renamed them outright "The Pepsi Generation." In 1966, Pepsi used a jingle called "Girlwatchers," which was designed to tap into a growing openness in the area of sexual mores. It became a top 40 hit. With its 1967 "Taste that Beats the Others Cold: Pepsi Pours it On" campaign, Pepsi then started tapping into a growing competitiveness in society. By the decade's end, Pepsi merged the two textualities—youth rebellion and affluence—with its 1969 campaign "You've Got a Lot to Live. Pepsi's Got a Lot to Give."

Throughout the 1970s and 1980s, Pepsi showed its resourcefulness in adapting to pop-culture trends more and more. Here are some examples. In 1973, the themes of freedom and youth tribalism that the hippie movement had spawned were encapsulated in its "Join the Pepsi People, Feelin' Free" campaign. In 1975, it adopted the theme of the growing challenges facing a constantly changing technological society in its "Pepsi Challenge" campaign. With its 1976 "Have a Pepsi Day" campaign, in which a little boy encounters puppies in ads and commercials, Pepsi wanted to show its own sensitivity towards society-wide concerns over childhood issues. Between 1979 and 1982, Pepsi mounted two highly successful campaigns—"Catch the Pepsi Spirit, Drink it In!" and "Pepsi's Got the Taste for Life"—that were cleverly designed to capture the growing egoism of the generation of the era, now characterized as the "Me Generation." In 1984–5 Pepsi was among the first brands to use pop-culture stars in its ad campaigns, reflecting the growing power of the media in society and the fact that young people of the era were the first generation to have grown up as "TV's babies." Michael Jackson declared Pepsi "The Choice of a New Generation," and Tina Turner, Gloria Estefan, Lionel Ritchie, Joe Montana, Dan Marino, Teri Garr, and Billy Crystal were featured in "New Generation" commercials on television. Michael J. Fox starred in the classic commercial "Apartment 10G." In 1987, Pepsi called itself "America's Choice," with Michael Jackson as the star of its episodic four-part Chase commercial.

The co-option of pop-culture figures became its dominant method of campaigning in 1990. Teen stars Fred Savage and Kirk Cameron were featured in commercials entreating their peers to join the "New Generation," and music legend Ray Charles grooved to the times with

"You Got the Right One, Baby, Uh-Huh!" Other celebrities declared "Gotta Have It and Been There, Done That, Tried That" on commercial slots, reflecting the growing ennui among affluent teenagers of the era. This campaign culminated in 1993 with basketball star Shaquille O'Neal exhorting his viewers to "Be Young, Have Fun." Between 1995 and 1997, with its "Nothing Else is a Pepsi" and "Security Camera" campaigns, the pop drink company showed itself as being unique among the competition, in line with a growing stress on individuality and self-identity in society. With "GeneratioNext," in which the Spice Girls were featured, Pepsi revamped its "Pepsi Generation" theme, with this clever bit of self-reference. In 1998, Pepsi's "Dancing Bears" campaign, with its humorous tone, tapped into a growing emphasis on sitcom-style behavior in social interaction. In 1999, tapping again into the power of pop-culture stars as the icons of society, Pepsi's "Joy of Cola" campaign featured such classic icons as Marlon Brando, Isaac Hayes, Aretha Franklin, and Jeff Gordon. Finally in 2001–2, the brand mounted a truly revealing campaign, showing the company's ability to reflect cultural groupthink. Ads and commercials blurted out that Pepsi was the drink that remains "forever young," mirroring the desire in society not only to stay and look healthier for a longer period of life, but also to act and think differently than "older" people.

As the above "time capsule" shows, ad campaigns are powerful ways of ensuring that products become part of social consciousness. There is little doubt that they affect how people perceive a brand. Pepsi was created as a medicinal drink—to aid digestion. But through its campaigns it has lost this meaning completely. It is now a pop drink, blending in with youth lifestyles. As Holt (2004: 2–3) aptly puts it: "Although the product has a name, a trademarked logo, unique packaging, and perhaps other unique design features, the brand does not yet truly exist" until it becomes part of society and develops a history for itself that meshes with the history of the society during the same period of time.

Ad campaigns are part of a process that allows brands to fabricate a history for themselves—a process that is intertwined with the larger history of pop culture. In the early 2000s, a TV commercial showed Britney Spears dressed in scenes that represented changes in fashion and music from the 1950s to the present time. As the times changed so did the soft drink. The two histories were one and the same. The social critic W. T. Anderson (1992: 125–30) calls such fabrications "pseudoevents," because they are planned for the sole purpose of creating a meaning for themselves. In the previous chapter, they were called "Just-So" stories.

In a fascinating book, titled *Twenty Ads that Shook the World* (2000), James Twitchell discusses 20 ad campaigns that have become part of social history. As he aptly puts it (2000: 8): "They got into our blood-stream." The 20 are worth reproducing and discussing here:

1   P. T. Barnum's ads (1870s)
2   E. Pinkham's "Vegetable Compound" (1880s)
3   Pear's Soap (1888)
4   Pepsodent's "Magic" campaign (1920s)
5   Listerine's "If you want the truth" campaign (1924)
6   Queensboro's use of radio (1920s)
7   New Haven Railroad's "The Kid in Upper 4" ad (1942)
8   De Beers' "A Diamond Is Forever" campaign (1948)
9   Hathaway's "Hathaway Man" campaign (1951)
10 Miss Clairol's "Does She or Doesn't She?" campaign (1955)
11 Marlboro cigarette's "Marlboro Man" campaign (1950s)
12 Anacin's "Hammer-in-the-Head" campaign (1950s)
13 Volkswagen's "Think Small" campaign (1962)
14 Coca-Cola's "Things Go Better with Coke" campaign (1964)
15 Linden B. Johnson's campaign for the presidency (1964)
16 Revlon's "Charlie" campaign (1970s–80s)
17 Absolut Vodka's "Larceny" campaign (1980s)
18 Apple's "1984" commercial (1984)
19 The advent of the infomercial (1995)
20 Nike's "Michael Jordan" campaign (1990s)

By way of annotation, I will summarize Twitchell's 20 ads. Observe the way in which each campaign has been deliberately embedded in the general culture.

The ads created by entrepreneur and circus operator P. T. Barnum (1810–91) in the 1870s introduced many of the techniques discussed in this book to create systems of signification for products. The Barnum ads introduced expressions such as the following into the lexicon of advertising and, by extension, into everyday discourse:

•   Don't miss this once-in-a-lifetime opportunity!
•   Limited edition at an unbelievably low price!
•   All items must go!
•   Not to be missed!

Lydia E. Pinkham's Vegetable Compound ad of the 1880s—a campaign designed to promote remedies for female uterine infections—was among the first to become integrated with the product label. Its logo of the grandmotherly Pinkham became a kind of cultural emblem that captured many people's fancy.

As one of the first to adopt a brand name, the Pear's Soap Company produced a truly captivating ad in 1888, on which the picture of a lonely child is displayed with the following accompanying text:

> A specialty for improving the complexion and preventing redness, roughness and chapping, recommended by Mrs Langtry, Madame Patti and obtained 15 international medals as a competition soap.

This "portrait of childhood" mirrored the maudlin sentimental view of childhood that prevailed in a society possessing Victorian values. The angelic face of the child nicely captured the view of children as innocent creatures.

In the 1920s, Pepsodent toothpaste mounted one of the first true modern ad campaigns featuring a man and a woman seated at a restaurant. It warned people that romance between two people was not possible without "pretty teeth":

> Magic
> Lies in pretty teeth
> Remove that film.

A similar scare tactic can be seen in Listerine's 1924 campaign which featured the slogan "If you want the truth—go to a child" and the picture of a child reacting adversely to the mother's bad breath. The mother was shown with her head turned slightly away from the child, so that the child would not get a whiff of her halitosis.

The use of radio to promote a product was initiated by the Queensboro Corporation in the 1920s. As mentioned previously, the radio commercial transformed advertising. With the accompaniment of catchy music, the employment of dialogue and other dramatic devices, the radio commercial gave the advertiser's message narrative and entertaining qualities that print could not possibly give to it. Entire radio programs became associated with products as a consequence.

New Haven Railroad's The Kid in Upper 4 ad of 1942 opened the door to "the strategy of drawing consumer attention away from the product, so that the negative aspects associated with a product could be ignored." The ad showed a young man in an upper berth, awake, pondering something; in the berth below him, two other young men could be seen sleeping. The text revealed what the youth in the upper berth was thinking—"leaving behind the taste of hamburgers" and "the pretty girl who writes so often." This strategy of the ad was to shift people's attention away from the lousy train service of the era. It worked effectively. Train use went up considerably after the ad campaign was mounted. The "kid in upper 4" became an icon—a subject of magazines such as *Life, Newsweek,* and *Time,* a character an MGM movie short, and the subject of a popular song. This ad showed clearly the extent to which advertising was starting to become integrated into the larger cultural system.

De Beers' 1948 campaign utilizing the catchy phrase "A Diamond Is Forever," utilized a WAG strategy linking love, marriage, and its diamonds. It is relevant to note that, in 2005 ads, de Beers has altered its signification system. In an age of high divorce rates and personal indulgence, the de Beer ads are designed to appeal to women with the financial means to subvert the "diamonds are a girl's best friend" tradition. The 1948 campaign portrayed the diamond ring as an engagement symbol. The subtext was a progression from love to engagement to marriage and living happily ever after. The new ad campaign is designed instead as a pitch to women directly, portraying a diamond ring as an expression of personal taste rather than as connected symbolically to courtship and marriage. The different ads in the campaign contained a different subtext—a diamond ring is something women can give to themselves without the heavy expectations of love and commitment. The body language of the models in the ads is sexually aggressive. In a traditional courtship situation, male and female roles are clearly defined: men buy and give rings; women receive and wear them. But as the tag line in the new ads claim, the time has come to do the following: "Women of the world, raise your right hand." The line is laden with multiple meanings. First, it is a play on the expression, "Workers of the world, unite!" a rallying cry for oppressed people. However, it also suggests that putting the ring on the right hand, rather than the left (the one reserved for engagement and wedding rings), women can declare their independence.

The decade of the 1950s brought with it the entrenchment of many contemporary advertising practices and the constant spread of branding. In 1951, Hathaway shirts were promoted as distinctive brands, entrenching the use of clothing brands as identifiers of personality, once and for all. Miss Clairol's highly successful "Does She or Doesn't She?" campaign of 1955, introduced the gossip technique into advertising. The creation of a fictitious character by Marlboro cigarettes, called the Marlboro Man in the 1950s, became a symbol of American manhood for a long period of time thereafter. And for many people, he remains so to this very day. The rugged, virile Marlboro Man beckons people to "come to where the flavour is."

The flavour is, of course, in "Marlboro country," which is a metaphor for America as a frontier where one can live "the carefree life of the cowboy." The Marlboro Man is a man of few words. He is the exemplar of the "strong silent cowboy"—an image that appeals to many men—and women.

Anacin showcased the power of suggestion by creating ads and com-mercials in the 1950s portraying pain inside the human head as comparable to the clanking sound made by a banging hammer and the harrowing sensation produced by an electric charge. This was a period in North America when awareness of stress and psychological-somatic states was increasing.

Volkswagen's incredibly successful "Think Small campaign" (1962) promoting its Beetle model, and Coca-Cola's similarly effective "Things Go Better with Coke" (1964) campaign, were classic examples of how a brand could co-opt social trends and integrate them into its textuality.

In 1964, aware of the success that advertising had reaped for Eisenhower before him, Linden B. Johnson's presidential campaign team decided to use an ad campaign designed to tap directly into the dominant fear of the era—extinction through the atomic bomb. The ad showed a little girl in separate frames—as in a comic book sequence. The girl was annihilated in the last frame by an atomic blast. The tag line, "We must love each other, or else die," completed the ad. Many political pundits claim, to this day, that it got Johnson elected.

Revlon's Charlie ads of the 1970s and 1980s were particularly effec-tive because they reflected trends brought about by the feminist movement of the era. One ad showed a female dressed in business attire, carrying a briefcase, and, in a clear reversal of roles, touching the derrière of a handsome young man. This "role-reversal" method left a permanent imprint on advertising technique. A 2002 Candie's perfume ad, for example, showed a female dressed only in bra and panties in a bathroom with the medicine cabinet open. In the cabinet the viewer could see two bottles of the perfume and a massive pile of condoms. The model in the ad had a sexually enticing gleam on her face.

Absolut Vodka's ingenious Larceny campaign of the 1980s showed how powerful images can be in promoting a brand's signification system. The ads in the campaign showed a lock on a chain that had obviously been broken. That image spoke volumes on its own—"Break loose," "Don't get caught," etc. Since then, Absolut Vodka, aware of the power of visual images, has employed some of the world's top photographic artists to construct their ads, blurring the line between art and brands significantly. On its website, the brand shows its "top 100 ads" proudly (see www.absolutad.com).

In Apple Computer's brilliant 1984 commercial, which was shown on January 22, 1984, during the third quarter of Super Bowl XVIII on television, the distinction between brands and art became even blurrier. Obviously evocative of George Orwell's *1984*, and directed by Ridley Scott, whose 1982 movie *Blade Runner* was already a cult classic at the time, the commercial won countless advertising awards and was characterized by culture historians as "the commercial that outplayed the game." Orwellian and other "1984-ish" themes have since then found their way into a host of ad campaigns, including one by Zenith (2001), that showed automatonic, depersonalized human robots walking all in tandem, without eyes, while a little girl who, with bright eyes, sees a new Zenith television set sitting on a column in the midst of this arid, spiritless, totalitarian world. The apparition and her childlike discovery of the apparition instantly humanize the mindless throng, as their eyes emerge as if by metamorphosis from a cocoon. In 2002, TV car commercials generally adopted the surrealistic feel of the computer screen as captured by the 1999 movie *The Matrix*. Such commercials attempted to create a feeling of "escape from reality," into a world of "total control."

The first infomercial appeared in 1995; since then, television channels promoting goods and services all day long have become commonplace throughout the world. Bluntly, these glorify consumerism. And, lastly, Nike's extremely successful Michael Jordan campaign of the 1990s established the practice of co-opting pop-culture figures as part of a "philosophy of life" associated with the brand, rather than as human props in a commercial promotional campaign.

It is no exaggeration to say that the history of modern Western culture is intrinsically interwoven with the history of brands. In looking back over the last century, it is obvious that the messages of advertisers and their textual styles have become intrinsic components of cultural lore. The evidence for this is unquestionable—in writing a historiography of modern-day culture one cannot avoid interweaving into it the historiography of brand advertising and of branding processes generally. Throughout the twentieth century, in fact, brand textualities and social trends mirrored and shaped each other. Table 5.6 illustrates the representation of women in ads for cosmetic products over the last century.

Through strategic ad campaigns, brands have, in fact, become part of history. As Anderson (1992: 126–7) aptly puts it, they have taken "the raw material of experience" refashioning it into stories. The brands retell the stories to us, and we call them reality.

Table 5.6 Representation of women in cosmetic ads

Period	Representation of women in ads
Early 1900s	Women had gained more independence, both socially and financially, and thus many more could afford cosmetics. With the advent of the nickel and dime store in the 1920s, women started being portrayed as beautiful goddesses (donning popular hairstyles of the era) on product packages, in ads, etc.
1930s and 1940s	The portrayal of women as sexually desirous was becoming common in cosmetic ads. Rosie the Riveter, with her sexy poses, was created as a "role model" for all women.
1950s	Images of partly clad women in ads became the norm. The power of the photographic image was unmistakable.
1960s–70s	Brands such as Revlon and Chanel further entrenched the image of the "sexual woman," with ads showing women as "goddesses" with perfect bodies.
1980s	The use of sexy women to sell everything, from cosmetics to cars to alcohol, increased dramatically.
1990s–2000s	Brands such as Calvin Klein emphasized the voluptuousness of the body, showcasing "idealized body images" of thin, attractive models.

POETIC LOGIC

The term "brand logic" is being used more often in place of "brand image" in the relevant literature to provide a conceptual framework to explain the "logic of branding." But, in my view, the more appropriate term is "poetic logic," a term coined by the Neapolitan philosopher Giambattista Vico. The word "logic" derives from the Greek *logos,* meaning both "word" and the "thought" it evokes. A product is something made in factories, in shops, etc. A brand, on the other hand, is a logical construct—a name evoking an unconscious system of thought. But the "logical reasoning" used is hardly deductive or rational; it is, rather, based on a poetic sense of the meaning nuances built into words. The underlying hypothesis I have woven throughout the previous chapters has been, in fact, that the whole branding phenomenon would not have occurred without the simple "poetic act" of naming products.

Vico defined poetic logic as the faculty of the mind that guides our attempts to make sense of things in his landmark treatise of 1725, *The New Science* (Bergin and Fisch 1984). It is an imaginative form of reasoning that allows us to understand the world on our own human terms. He suggested that we can gain an understanding of how this form of reasoning unfolds by studying one of its most common products—metaphor. As remarkable as that insight was, it is only today that metaphor has finally started to catch the attention of linguists and psychologists.

Brands are, essentially, metaphors in the Vichian sense. As such, they become themselves constructs for further rhetorical processes in society. This can be seen in a fairly concrete way in the tendency of brands themselves to become part of what can be called "social logic"—an unconscious system of reasoning and inference that is tied to the rhetorical values of the brand names. In a phrase, brands make poetic sense. It is thus little wonder to find that often specific brand names have become general words for the products—a rhetorical process known more specifically as "metonymy." Table 5.7 lists some common cases in point.

Table 5.7 Brand names as metonymic sources of product names

Brand name	Now stands generally for. . .
Cola (Coca-Cola Co.)	a carbonated soft drink
Hoover	a vacuum cleaner
Jell-o (Kraft Co.)	gelatin dessert
Kleenex	a facial tissue
Popsicle (Good Humor-Breyers Ice Cream Co.)	a colored, flavored ice confection with one or two flat sticks for a handle
Post-it Note (Minnesota Mining and Manufacturing Co.)	any adhesive paper used as a memorandum
Q-tips (Pond's)	a cotton-tipped swab
Saran Wrap (Dow Chemical Co.)	a thermoplastic resin derived from vinyl compounds and used to make packaging films, fittings, and bristles and as a fiber in various heavy fabrics
Scotch Tape (Minnesota Mining and Manufacturing Co.)	any adhesive tape
Styrofoam (Dow Chemical Co.)	a light, resilient polystyrene plastic
Thermos (Top Thermo Manufacturing)	a vacuum bottle or insulated container
Twizzler (Hershey Foods)	a liquorice candy in the form of a spiral stick
Vaseline (Pond's)	a petroleum jelly
Walkman (Sony)	a portable radio/cassette player equipped with earphones
Xerox (Xerox Corp)	a photocopy or photocopying in general

The dominance of these brand names does not necessarily entail ultimate power. Sometimes, it can work against certain brands in the short term, since consumers might be willing to buy a cheap or supermarket's own cotton-tipped swab that they refer to (on their shopping list) simply as "Q-tips" (see Wright 1997). However, this metonymical phenomenon is striking.

Poetic logic is evidence that we use our imagination in tandem with our senses to understand the world. Poets, artists, and mathematicians have always known this and expressed it in their works. Words are, as Vico characterized them, "fables in brief," telling stories about their referents that are imbued with narrative and historical meanings tied to their values as signs. In a phrase, brands are powerful signs because they are imbued with poetic logic. They are not offshoots of rational deduction; they are consequences of the same kind of imaginative thinking that characterizes poetry. It is thus little wonder to find that (as we saw in the previous chapter) the brand marketers use the exact same kinds of techniques and devices that poets use in creating textualities for their products.

A poetic logic is indigenous to a culture and it is often one of the chief markers of a specific culture. As we have seen, brand management has employed poetic logic in order to close any gap between culture and brand, to raise the profile of a brand to a level where the culture surrounding it becomes itself branded. In the next chapter, we will encounter an inevitable consequence of the branding of culture: the extension of the poetic logic of brands on a global scale.

6

BRAND
GLOBALIZATION

Villages, unlike towns, have always been ruled by conformism, isolation, petty surveillance, boredom and repetitive malicious gossip about the same families. Which is a precise enough description of the global spectacle's present vulgarity.

Guy Debord (1931–)

The Canadian communications theorist, Marshall McLuhan (1911–80), predicted in the 1950s that the spread of electronic media would eventually turn the culturally fragmented world into one electronic Global Village where American brands, from Coca-Cola to McDonald's restaurants, would become, *ipso facto*, "global brands." With the advent of satellite television and the internet, McLuhan's prophetic vision has become a reality. The Global Village today is, as McLuhan envisaged, a virtual community where branding seems to be the dominant semiotic process—a fact that has led to reactionary movements and attacks of all kinds.

The purpose of this final chapter is to take a look at the implications that brand globalization entails, now that metatextuality has become a global reality because of the internet. The Global Village is, as social activists Thomas Frank (1997) and Naomi Klein (2000) argue, one shaped primarily by the lifestyle images of brand culture. Brand-name clothing is fast becoming global fashion, brand-name automobiles are creating the same kinds of symbolic values in the minds of people across the globe. In this way, single individuals, of any nation or group,

can now feel that they are participants in a larger social community—
a "community of man [sic]" extolled by brands such as Coca-Cola (with
its universal brotherhood campaign) and Benetton (with its united
colors of humanity campaigns). All each individual has to do is wear the
right kind of clothes, listen to the right kind of music, and talk the right
kind of talk.

The main focus in this book has been to describe and discuss the semiotics of branding—from the creation of a name and logo for a product
to the ways in which brand imagery is ensconced into cultural content
through advertising and partnerships with the media. In this chapter, I
will look at how the branding process has spread throughout the Global
Village and then comment on the rise of anti-brand movements that have
arisen in that very village.

GLOBAL BRANDS

The globalization of brands can be traced back to the the late 1960s
(Frank 1997). That was the period in time when the marketers decided
it was in its best interest not to fight images of youth insurgency, but
rather to embrace them outright, creating an "imagined youth community" through which all people could come together and establish a
common identity. It is imagined because the members do not know their
fellow members, yet in the minds of each one exists the image of their
unity. Brand-name recognition became the passport to this imagined
community.

The main strategy of this early "if-you-can't-beat-them-join-them"
approach was the development of an advertising style that mocked
consumerism and advertising itself. The strategy worked beyond expectations. Through advertising images, being young and rebellious came
to mean having a "cool look"; being anti-establishment and subversive
came to mean wearing "hip clothes"; and so on. The corporate leaders
had cleverly "joined the revolution," so to speak, by deploying media
images of youthful rebellion to market their goods and services. "Young"
and "different" became the two key words of the new advertising and
marketing lexicon, coaxing people into buying branded products, not
because they necessarily needed them, but simply because they were
new, cool, hip. The system of signification of this clever marketing
strategy allowed consumers to believe that what they bought transformed
them into ersatz revolutionaries without having to pay the social price of
true nonconformity and dissent.

The images of cool that the brands had co-opted quickly spread across
the globe through television and other media channels. By the mid-

1970s, the whole industrialized world was arguably becoming one "cool village," with everyone singing the same kinds of songs, dancing to the same kinds of music, wearing the same brands of clothing, and drinking Coke and Pepsi. The Global Village was starting to morph into a global brand culture.

Brand advertising had succeeded, more than any economic process or sociopolitical movement, in promoting and ensconcing a global community, albeit an imaginary one. By proposing marketplace solutions to virtually all social problems, branding has emerged as a form of persuasive ideology in itself. Perhaps, as some social activists warn, we do indeed live in a world conjured up by lifestyle ads and TV commercials. Yet it is far too easy to blame rampant consumerism for all our social ills. We must not forget that human-made systems may, in the end, be reflexes of innate human tendencies. One of these is the so-called "pleasure principle," as philosopher John Locke (1632–1704) called it— namely, instinctual drive to seek maximum pleasure or gratification and minimum pain. According to Freudian psychology, the principle originates in the libido and is the force that governs the id. Without necessarily embracing a Freudian perspective outright, there is little doubt that the pleasure principle is what probably directs a large percentage of human behavior and shapes human needs. It is, as Stuart Ewen aptly puts it, a tendency "that is closely interwoven with modern patterns of survival and desire" (1988: 20).

The images that suffuse life in the Global Village are, in actual fact, geared towards the achievement of pleasure through the acquisition of products. But therein lies the paradox of modern life—pleasures and desires can never truly be satisfied by means of consumption. The warnings come not only from religious communities, but also from the social scientific research domain, although the question remains: to what extent are such warnings objectively justifiable? Is advertising to be blamed for causing virtually everything that ails modern cultures, from a spiraling growth of obesity to street violence? Are media moguls the shapers of behavior that so many would claim they are today? Has advertising spawned the contemporary form of ennui? Are common folk today "victims" of media messages, as Key (1989: 13) suggests, who "scream and shout hysterically at rock concerts and later in life at religious revival meetings?" Media representations, like all kinds of representations, do indeed play a role in shaping behavior and groupthink. But, even though we might mindlessly absorb the messages promulgated constantly by the image-makers of the Global Village, and although these may have some subliminal effects on our behavior, we accept media images, by and large, only if they suit our already established preferences. As Freedman (2002) has recently argued, after assessing the relevant scientific literature on the effects of media on human behavior, we will never be able to say what these effects really are.

It is more accurate to say, in my view, that the images that the brand–media partnership produces on a daily basis reinforce lifestyle models that are already present in society. Brand companies are more intent on co-opting and reinforcing lifestyle behaviors than in spreading commercially risky innovations. The strategy of branding cultural content is not in itself disruptive of the value systems of the cultural mainstream; rather, it is reflective of shifts and tendencies already present in it. If branding has become psychologically effective, then, it is primarily because it taps into deeply-ingrained proclivities—especially the pleasure principle.

The establishment of the Global Village has been made possible by technology, starting already in the Renaissance with the advent of print technology, making print materials affordable through mass production and, as a consequence, spreading print literacy to the masses. Print literacy impels people to separate the maker of knowledge from the knowledge made, since the maker is not present when the reading process occurs. And this in turn leads to the perception that knowledge can exist on its own, spanning time and distance. Because of this, McLuhan characterized the emerging world shaped by print literacy as the "Gutenberg Galaxy," after the German printer Johan Gutenberg (c. 1400–68), the inventor of movable type. Through books, newspapers, pamphlets, and posters, McLuhan argued, the printed word became, after the fifteenth century, the primary means for the propagation of knowledge and ideas. More importantly, given the fact that print mater-ials could cross political boundaries, the printing press set in motion the globalization of culture. Paradoxically, as McLuhan (1962) observed, this process did not simultaneously lead to the elimination of all the distinct cultures that had previously existed. On the contrary, he claimed that "tribal tendencies" continued to resonate within people, creating even further tensions between peoples.

By the start of the twentieth century, the great advances made in print technology had brought about standardization in the conduct of various human activities, from diplomacy to scientific method. But the techno-logical event that truly made the Global Village the reality that it is today was the astounding advances in the science of electronics and, a little later in the century, in computer science. Print technology opened up the possibility of founding a "world civilization"; electronic and digital technologies have brought that possibility closer and closer to realization.

In today's "Digital Galaxy," the constant images seen on television and on computer screens have become the images of people across the globe.

They are powerful because they are signs that, unlike human pure computational data, cannot be neatly evaluated as true or false or pigeon-holed into distinct slots. They are emotional artifacts, to which people react as a community, even if it is an imaginary one. With those images, many conflicts, wars, and horrific cases of poverty would go unnoticed. Digital technology has brought these situations literally "into focus," stimulating activism or, at the very least, human concern and empathy. So, while the Global Village may have had some purportedly deleterious effects on the human psyche (at least according to some social critics), it has not stifled human empathy or altruism.

Needless to say, the Global Village has also been good for business, providing the electronic means for spreading brand imagery through the world and, thus, for providing the conditions for brands to achieve global status. A casebook example of a brand that has been successful in spreading its signification system in the global marketplace is Lux Toilet Soap, whose slogan is "The toilet soap of the stars." Lux (Latin for "light") has been a top-selling soap for over seven decades across the globe. Using well-known Hollywood stars along with local cinema and television stars to promote its products, the brand has guaranteed itself a niche in the global marketplace, promoting itself as being "global" and "community-based" at the same time. It is this double-brand identity that secures placement in the global marketplace.

Two other textbook cases are McDonald's and Disney—both of which have reached multinational status and are, practically, household names throughout the globe. The sociologist Bryman (2004) even sees their influence as having been instrumental in reshaping world culture. He refers to "McDonaldization" as the process "by which the principles of the fast-food restaurant are coming to dominate more and more sectors of American society as well as the rest of the world" (Bryman 2004: 25) and "Disneyization" as the correlative process "by which the principles of the Disney theme parks are coming to dominate more and more sectors of American society as well as the rest of the world" (Bryman 2004: 26). Both processes are consequences of the "double branding strategy" adopted first by Lux—the strategy of blending into the global and the local culture in tandem (see also Ritzer 2004 on this point). One marketing study, cited by Eric Schlosser (2001: 34), found that the golden arches are now more recognizable across the globe than the Christian cross. As a symbol of unabashed American capitalism, it is little wonder that in recent years the fast-food eatery has been the target of demonstrations, vandalism, and attacks throughout the globe. People are sometimes driven to react to symbols more than they do to social realities.

As the last statement implies, the success of Lux, McDonald's, Coca-Cola, and Disney is explainable in straightforward semiotic terms. By co-opting local signification systems and blending them with more global ones, the brands have become true symbolic signs in the Peircean sense—signs forged through the channel of cultural convention. McDonald's has done this in part by allowing its menu to vary according to religious and social traditions across the world. In India, for example, the eatery served "Vegetable McNuggets" and a "Mutton Maharaja Mac" in the early 2000s—culinary adaptations that are necessary in a country where Hindus do not eat beef, Muslims do not eat pork, and Jains eat no meat at all.

This "blending of signification systems" is the strategy that turns products into global brands. Global branding is a sign-based process that generates signification systems that allow people to accept the brand as an aspect of their life schemes, allowing them to see themselves as members of local and global communities at once. Success in the global marketplace is measurable, in fact, on the ability of a brand to transform itself into a "global identity."

CO-OPTION

The word "co-option" has been used throughout this book to explain how branding comes about. The word was foregrounded in cultural studies and social science generally by Thomas Frank in his pivotal 1997 book, *The Conquest of Cool*. Frank proposed it to describe the dominant strategy of the big brands in the 1960s to appropriate the symbols of counterculture lifestyle as their own, adapting and recycling them into society at large through a refashioning of their semiotic value. Counterculture clothing and fashion were thus quickly converted into mainstream fashion by many clothing companies such as Levi Jeans; counterculture music style became the code adopted by the big record brands, making it mainstream music style, etc. By the decade's end, this strategy led to the crystallization of a social mindset whereby every individual could feel that he or she was "part of the scene," as mentioned above.

Co-option is now the primary means by which branding occurs. Keeping in step with trends in the (imaginary) youth culture is the basic approach by which brand identity can be kept fresh and vibrant. This produces gradual, but constant, alterations to the content and form of brand textuality. An enhanced definition of co-option would take into account the action-reaction of several factors of change in the environment in which branding occurs—namely, factors related to changes in values, technology, economic outlook, marketplace competition, political governance, corporate philosophy, and other broader changes in the Global Village. The textuality of any well-thought advertising campaign will reflect influences from these domains, not just the imaginary youth culture. At the same time, pioneering brands are likely to react on this environment and amplify the trend (be it technological, economic, etc.) by appropriate textuality.

As mentioned, co-option crystallized in the context of the hippie movement against the "military-economic complex" of American society. Campaigns, such as the Pepsi Generation (with the slogan "Join the Pepsi Generation") and the Coke "Universal Brotherhood" ones, directly incorporated the images, rhetoric, and symbolism of the counterculture movement into their textualities. The Coke campaign especailly showed the extent to which the counterculture message had become branded. "Universal harmony" through drinking Coke became the subliminal thread woven into its campaign of the early 1970s. The Dodge Rebellion and Oldsmobile Youngmobile campaigns followed the soft drink ones, etching into the nomenclature of the car brands themselves the powerful connotations of youth rebellion and defiance. Even a sewing company, alas, came forward to urge on people to join its own type of surrogate revolution, with its slogan "You don't let the establishment make your world; don't let it make your clothes." In effect, by claiming to "join the revolution," the big brands created the real revolution in the domain of marketing. This is why, since the late 1960s, the worlds of advertising, marketing, and entertainment have become totally intertwined with youth lifestyle, both responding and contributing to the rapid fluctuations in social trends. It should go without saying, of course, that young people are also an important target market with disposable income.

Today, the inhabitants of the Global Village, which novelist Douglas Coupland (1991) has perceptively called "Global Teens" (regardless of their age), have appropriated "cool images" so completely that many of them are no longer recognized as artifacts of co-option. The end result has been a further obliteration of the crucial emotional difference that traditional cultures have maintained between the social categories of young and old. This is why nowadays the rhetoric of youth is quickly transformed by advertising textuality into the rhetoric of all; why the fashion trends of the young are recycled and marketed shortly after their invention as the fashion styles of all; and why the fluctuating musical aesthetics of the youth culture are quickly incorporated into the musical aesthetics of society at large. Adolescent cool has, in effect, become the social norm. The many self-proclaimed "rebels" and "revolutionaries" of the 1960s' counterculture, who genuinely thought they were bringing about a radical change to the mainstream consumerist culture, ended up becoming the incognizant trendsetters of the very culture they deplored, providing it with features of lifestyle and discourse that the brand power brokers have, since the 1960s, been able to adapt and recycle into society at large.

In actual fact, the origin of the co-option process, with its emphasis on being, staying, thinking, and looking young at any age, can be traced right back to the first decades of the twentieth century, when a gradually increasing economic affluence in Western society at large set this cultural process in motion. For the first time in history, a single economic system was capable of guaranteeing a certain level of affluence to increasingly larger segments of society. With more wealth and leisure time at their disposal, common people became more inclined to live the good life. And with the economic capacity to ameliorate their chances of staying healthier, and thus of living much longer than previous generations, a desire to preserve a youthful look for a much longer period of life started to define the collective state of mind. This desire was nurtured by the messages that circulated in society through radio and print advertising in the early part of the century—messages that became more persuasive and widespread with the advent of television as a form of textuality in the early 1950s. By the 1960s, the desire to be "young" not only meant the desire to stay and look healthier for a longer period of life, but also to act and think differently from older people. Being old meant being a part of the corrupt and morally fossilized "establishment," as the consumerist way of life was called by the counterculture dissidents.

For many today, wearing Nike, Lacoste, the Gap, or whatever brand is "in," is what defines cool, not counterculture symbolism. These words now designate lifestyle chic, not social protest, and their connotations are being set not by counterculture rebels, but by advertisers and marketers. The semantics of the new counterculture code is that the right "look," the right "talk," the right "walk" are what make someone cool and hip. The "conquest of cool" by the brands, as Frank (1997) characterizes it, has thus bestowed upon the imagery and textuality of products the same kind of authority that the more traditional symbolic forms and texts had in previous eras. But unlike previous privileged discourses, the grammar of cool exalts and inculcates Epicurean values, not wisdom or cultural evolution. It classifies human beings into "taste groups," "lifestyle groups," "market segments," and the like. In the semantic system of this language, the individual human being is hardly envisioned as a being with a unique individuality, but rather as a nameless entity whose behavior can be inferred from the laws of Gaussian statistics, and thus easily manipulated. As Frank emphasizes, the conquest of cool has had a radical surreptitious effect on the psychology and sociology of the contemporary world.

Co-option was the perfect intellectual antidote to the real threat to consumerist economics posed by counterculture ideology. As the social critic Ewen has aptly put it, the business world discovered fortuitously in that era how to incorporate the powerful images of youth protest into "the most constantly available lexicon from which many of us draw the visual grammar of our lives" (1988: 20). That lexicon allows the brands to easily build new semantic bridges between the product and the consumer's consciousness. This is why the constant craving for new items of consumption is no longer perceived as an aberration, but as part of the search for happiness, success, status, or beauty. It has, as mentioned in the previous chapter, its own poetic logic.

For the sake of historical accuracy, it should be mentioned that, in general, youth culture and the hippie movement in particular in the US was hardly seen at first as a threat to the socioeconomic order. It became a concern only after the Chicago Democratic Convention of 1968 turned violent. It was at that crucial turning point that the business world became alarmed at the direction that the youth culture was taking. The co-option strategy that the advertising and marketing moguls devised was hardly an option; it was a drastic survival measure. Having nurtured the blossoming of the youth culture in the 1950s, the business world had become suddenly afraid that the socioeconomic order it had fashioned for itself, which had become highly dependent on the buying patterns of adolescents, would crumble under the weight of the hippie revolution. The manifestation of youth rebellion shown at the Chicago convention was unique in history, and it put a scare into those who had invested the economic future of the Western world in teenagers. In effect, by the late 1960s, with the threat of adolescents truly growing up and rejecting the capitalist system, the co-option strategy was a desperation measure. It worked because it ingeniously effaced even more than in the previous decade the dividing line between young and old.

The co-option strategy turned social criticism into clothing fashion, hairstyles, and musical forms, making the business world itself a partner of the hippies in bringing about change. Even the hippies knew that being revolutionary entailed being cool, hence the ultimate hypocrisy of the counterculture movement, moving along exactly as Madison Avenue wanted it to after the Chicago Convention. The only authentic rebel of the counterculture, Frank (1997) claims, was Abbie Hoffman, whose book titled *Steal this Book* (1996)—a handbook of how to survive stealing that Hoffman wanted readers to shoplift from stores—was the only kind of subversive gesture that was truly hostile and menacing to the corporate world order. The other revolutionaries were, as it turned out, really adolescents doing no more than waging battles with their parents and with one another.

The lesson learned from the success of the co-option strategy by big business is that the road into any marketplace is paved not only by economic savvy, but also by cultural savvy. A brand that understands how to tap into "global cool" is the one that is most likely to gain a niche in the global marketplace. In a sense, the Global Village has brought about a demise of the original form of capitalism, intended for the benefit of the bourgeoisie, and has transformed itself into one of market populism, a place where a Bill Gates and his legion of cool tattooed geeks can claim to look after the interests of the "common guy like them." Such a claim would be seen for what it is—a hypocritical stance of market populists—if not for the fact that the global marketplace had not already become, before the Bill Gates' era, not just a place of business and commerce, but also an imaginary community in which values, opinions, and ideas are put forward for recognition or debate.

Today, the heterogeneous lifestyles associated with the many youth subcultures that make up the highly fragmented "media cosmos," from "hip-hop," to "alternative," to "punk," to "rave," or to whatever, are hardly perceived by the consumerist oligarchy as posing a serious threat to the economic order. They might be perceived as bizarre or weird, but they are not seen as subversive or as part of a youth coup d'état. The counterculture reformers saw the Western world's blatant materialism as having created the social conditions that ineluctably induced the all-pervading sense of alienation and of rootlessness that Western people so commonly feel. Materialism, they claimed, had undermined the common values shared by common folk. A breakdown of these values due to extreme forms of materialism, they believed, led to a loss of social stability and to individual feelings of anxiety and dissatisfaction. The hippies felt that they were doing something meaningful to combat alienation. They fought against misery and oppression. They sought to reestablish the spiritual over the material. But as it turned out, they ended up being the unwitting instruments of the materialists. The hippies did not pull the plug on capitalism; they merely altered its approach and unwittingly gave it new dynamism.

In a more recent critique, Frank (2000) has gone one step further in his assessment of the ability of big business to tap into social trends through their institutionalization of cultural savvy. The brands are, he suggests, the new anthropologists of culture, attempting to put a virtual end to social evolution. Frank's argument should be challenged on this point, however. Co-option could not have worked as successfully as it did in the first place unless there already existed in the "social genes" of the Western world a built-in tendency towards consumerism. The roots of the hippie revolution were, arguably, to be found in human sentiments—by an abhorrence of social injustice, by a disgust over discrimination against specific groups (such as African–Americans and women), and so on—not by a total aversion to capitalism. Sooner or later, the same sentiments will provoke other movements, other revolutions. It is ironical to note that the very images of Western capitalism that the hippies deplored were adopted by the youths of communist countries two decades later as they successfully brought down communism. Indeed, branded commodities such as Levi jeans and Coca-Cola were highly valued symbols of rebellion in communist countries up until the fall of the Soviet Union. That, in my view, is the greatest paradox of all and something that neither Frank nor anyone else can really fathom.

If product branding has been successful, it is because it has understood the needs of human beings and exploited them, in the same way that various other ideologies have, from the religious to the political. A critique of capitalism without taking the larger context of human ideologies is ultimately vacuous. Branding, moreover, is a social process that goes beyond product economics. Take, as an example, the case of the late "king of rock and roll," Elvis Presley. Elvis is now a full-fledged brand, which includes as part of its metatextuality reissues of his music, movies, and brand-name products: socks, sweaters, lipstick, pencils, sodas, and pajamas. Clearly, there is a capitalist imperative involved in the sale of such commodities. However, Elvis, as the nodal point of a number of values, emotions, and human investments is more than a simple product. Cases of similar branding have occurred throughout the modern world, from rock stars to sports personalities and even artists.

One interesting footnote to the Elvis brand is its longevity. Decades after his death in 1977, Elvis remains a cultural icon. Indeed, all iconic brands stay around for a while, even after death of the individuals involved, including political leaders such as John F. Kennedy and Martin Luther King, as well as socialite figures, such as the late Princess Diana. Any critique of branding that does not take this broader picture into account is, as pointed out, useless. Moreover, people seem to like brands in the same way that they like any artifact. Consider again the case of co-branding discussed in the previous chapter. The inclusion of coffee shops such as Starbucks in bookstores is something that people can relate to in a socio-symbolic fashion. This dimension to a co-branding event has even been the target of several recent movies. The 1998 film *You've Got Mail* is a case in point. The "coffee scene" in that movie can be experienced almost everywhere. It is the defining social code in the world inhabited by the actors. The coffee bar in the bookstore offers a variety of flavors and preparations, mirroring the flavors and modalities of that code. As Tom Hanks explains in an e-mail to Meg Ryan:

> The whole purpose of places like Starbucks is for people, with no decision-making ability what-so-ever, to make six decisions, just to buy one cup of coffee! Short, tall, light, dark. Café, decaf, low fat, non-fat, etc . . . So people don't know what they are doing or what the hell they are getting, and only for $2.95, not just a cup of coffee but an absolute defining sense of self. Tall, decaf cappuccino.

Analogously, in the 2000 film *What Women Want*, Mel Gibson meets up with Marisa Tomei in the coffee shop where she works. Gibson orders a "moccachino" with extra foam. Tomei then asks him to specify the size he wants: "tall" or "grande." At this point there is a pause, allowing us to realize that the question is laden with sexual innuendoes. Gibson proceeds to tell Tomei that he is getting a promotion: "Come with me, celebrate, I'll buy you a cup of coffee." She replies: "Memo, for you: I work in a coffee shop!" Her reply concisely summarizes the foregoing discussion—namely, that people are what make branding what it is, not just the corporations. The success of branding is not just the result of the clever marketing strategies of marketers. It requires the complicity of consumers.

CULTURE JAMMING

In the last decade or so, there have been calls for boycotts of global brands throughout the world. Together with demonstrations and attacks against brand outlets (such as McDonald's), it is obvious that the success of the branding movement has spawned an anti-branding one.

Among the activist anti-brand groups and ideologies, the most interesting one from a semiotic perspective is the so-called "culture-jamming" movement, since its approach is to unmask the signification systems of brands so that more and more people can gain critical understanding of the images that float through them on a daily basis, and thus to provide people with crucial "cognitive filters" for screening branded messages. Mainly led by Adbusters (see www.adbusters.org), the culture-jamming endeavor revolves around consciousness-raising in respect of brands and advertising (see Klein 2000). One of the main means it has used for this purpose is the production of alternative advertisements, some of which are free-standing artworks rather than items circulated in a marketing environment, which parody or bluntly draw attention to strategies of the purveyors of global brands. Ultimately, however, as Adbusters claims, the "aim is to topple existing power structures and forge a major shift in the way we will live in the 21st century." In a sense, the current-day culture-jamming movement takes its impetus from the common view of consumerist culture as a huge distraction factory, aimed at uprooting the traditional forms of art and meaning-making. But such a position suggests that there was a halcyon period when art and meaning-making were not driven by elitism and social differences and that meaning-making was not severely limited in scope and audience. In fact, the distraction factory has, actually, had a beneficial effect on human cultural evolution by engendering a "democratization of art." By this I mean that, today, anyone with the necessary spending power can buy a CD of any piece of (available) classical music, a DVD of any classic movie, or acquire any in-print novel he or she desires—opportunities that were not available in a purported "idyllic" pre-pop-culture era to which culture jammers seem so nostalgically attached. Even television, with its focus on distraction, has a good side to it. It provides comfort and companionship for many people, especially elderly ones, during long solitary evenings, not to mention stimulating social commentary in the form of documentaries and news programs that have, frequently, mobilized social activism.

Semioticians such as Roland Barthes have blamed the brand–media partnership for inculcating materialistic values. Since the late 1950s, "brand and media bashing" has become common from both the right and the left of the intellectual and ideological spectrum. Global branding, advertising, and marketing are blamed for causing everything from street violence and family breakups to philosophical nihilism throughout the world. Even the present author recently joined the fray in a study of the "juvenilization of culture" (Danesi 2003). But are the critics (including the present one) right?

The view that specific cultural activities and forms of representation influence behavior is, actually, an old view. Already in the ancient world, the Greek historian Herodotus (c. 484–425 BCE) claimed that Egyptians thought differently from the Greeks because they wrote their books from right to left rather than from left to right, as was the Greek practice. Herodotus thus put forward the notion that the characteristics of the codes used by a culture to carry out its representational activities influenced how the members of that culture understood the world. A similar view was articulated by the fourteenth-century Algerian scholar Ibn Khaldun (1332–1406), who wrote a truly fascinating treatise in which he noted that the subtle behavioral differences that existed between nomadic and city-dwelling Bedouins were due to their differences in language and in how they used such differences to speak about reality. The same type of view was reiterated centuries later by Johann Gottfried von Herder (1744–1803), Wilhelm von Humboldt (1767–1835), Georg Wilhelm Friedrich Hegel (1770–1831) and Martin Heidegger (1889–1976). These intellectuals claimed that worldview is a product of culture and influences from the social environment.

The culture-jamming movement has taken the view of such intellectuals seriously, believing that it can turn the tables around, by attacking the social environment through what can be called "counter-signification." So, for example, on posters for Coca-Cola, the caption "It's the Real Thing" might be modified by a culture jammer (through defacement) to read "It's the Real Thing that can harm your health and ruin the world." It must be noted, however, that culture jammers are usually more humorous and incisive than this example allows. In a semiotic sense, the culture jammer takes the connotation out of the message, rendering it literal and thus openly revelatory. The argument put forward by the culture jammers is based on the view that the kinds of content that brand promotion activities contain have perverting effects on people, because of their metaphorical content.

If the culture jammers are correct, then the "Big Brother" that George Orwell (1903–50) described in his 1949 novel *1984* has, seemingly, taken over the globe. However, many questions arise with regard to the culture jammer's overall outlook. After all, it has always been easy to blame big business and the media for thwarting the more "noble goals" of life that people would otherwise purportedly pursue. This would mean, of course, that the "blamers" have some secret knowledge of what those goals are and, more importantly, of why people should pursue them. But, as at any other period of human history, it is difficult, if not impossible, to pinpoint what is "ennobling" and what is "demeaning" from the current slate of human activities, aspirations, and concepts.

Some culture jammers also link shopping addiction with brand advertising. It is, of course, true to an extent, but not completely. People go to malls not just to shop, but also to engage in a form of socialization. The mall has replaced the town square and the piazza (Berger 2005: 99–109). It is relevant to note that, in a recent study of malls, Paco Underhill (2004) has demonstrated that the mall is now as part of everyday life as was any other meeting locus of the past, and a locus for self-expression through shopping, as Danziger (2004) argues. Some may not like this aspect of modern-day lifestyle, but it is a fact of life for many who clearly do.

The consequences of the reckless globalization of mass manufacturing and mass marketing, especially for so many frivolous products are, needless to say, greatly worrisome, with global warming and the depletion of the earth's natural resources reaching dangerous levels, not to mention the deepening of existing inequalities related to policies and conditions engendering the social exclusion of various peoples (Munck 2004). But are the brands to be blamed exclusively for all this? Is everyone else an innocent victim of their clever manipulations?

The culture jammers' view that the brand–media partnership is indelibly altering human psychology is actually a version of the so-called "Hypodermic Needle Theory" that was highly popular in the 1980s, when the culture-jamming movement started gaining momentum. It claims that media representations are capable of directly swaying minds with the same kind of impact a drug-filled hypodermic needle has on the body. The popularity and spread of junk food is often cited in support of this theory. Promoted by effective advertising campaigns, junk food has become part of the common diet. But the consequences on health have been disastrous. The inordinate consumption of junk food is, in fact, one of the main factors contributing to the rise in obesity (Schlosser 2001). And this has created a psychologically damaging situation for those who become obese, since their body image is at odds with the ultra-slim body images that the media perpetrate as the norm for attractiveness. This disjunction of fact and image, which psychologists call "cognitive dissonance," has likely generated culture-based crazes, such as dieting and fitness crazes.

But the hypodermic-needle view ignores the historical record. The ravages of overeating or undereating are not just contemporary phenomena, induced by exposure to the media. They have always been symptomatic of the excesses of affluent lifestyles in the case of the former and of strictly religious ones in the case of the latter. Fasting, for instance, has been practiced for centuries in connection with religious ceremonies. Originally, it was one of a number of rites in which physical activities were reduced or suspended, resulting in a state of quiescence symbolically comparable to death, or to the state preceding birth. Fasts were also part of fertility rites in primitive ceremonies. Modern-day diet crazes are not that far removed from fasting practices of the past. They usually involve processes of denial and righteousness which are clearly analogous.

Ultimately, the culture-jamming movement raises the question of what content is "kosher," so to speak, and, more importantly, *who* has the right (if anyone) of deciding what goes into the cultural system. The danger in attacking brand representations as "harmful" and other kinds of representations as "acceptable" is in setting up an ideological hierarchy. Moreover, *pace* the "Hypodermic Needle Theory" in which the only individuals who notice the interests behind brand promotion are a clerisy of social theorists, most people can easily distinguish between what is appropriate for living a meaningful life and what is not. It is useless, in my view, to propose drastic measures to censor or repress media expressions of any kind in order to counteract any purported hypodermic-needle effect. For one thing, media messages produce such an effect only if individuals are already predisposed toward their content; and for another, brand moguls will find ways around such measures.

More and more groups in America, Canada, Britain, and other consumerist cultures have started to suggest censorship as a means of gaining control over the levers of the media, and especially over the advertising messages that permeate the entire social order. But the answer to the dilemma of branded culture is not to be found in censorship or in any form of state control. Even if it were possible in democratic societies to control the contents of the media and the promotional activities of the brands, this would hardly solve the "problems of humanity." Immunization against any deleterious effects that the brand–media partnership may be having on us is, in my view, to become aware of the signification systems that are spread by this partnership. In this way, we will be better able, as individuals, to fend off any undesirable effects that such texts may cause.

Admittedly, this is the ultimate objective of the culture jammers, too. They are a loose global network of media activists aiming to change the way that the media and corporate institutions wield power. In *Culture Jam* (2000), the Canadian founder of the movement, Kalle Lasn, makes a persuasive case against the globalization of consumerist culture. To combat the growing acceptance of branded messages in a Just-So way, Lasn founded *Adbusters* magazine in 2000, which led to the organization of the same name introduced above. The magazine itself was an early example of the culture-jamming enterprise of satirizing brand–media activities and exposing them for what they are—clever ruses to get people to buy things. Lasn believes that corporate America is no longer a country, but one overarching "brand" shaped by the cult of celebrity and the spectacles that sustain it. Culture and marketing have, according to Lasn, become one and the same.

Lasn's fears are not unfounded. There are a small number of colossal media conglomerates that run the global economy (Disney, Time Warner, Bertelsmann, Viacom, News Corporation, PolyGram, NBC, MCA, Sony, etc.). Global advertising is now under the control of, basically, a handful of advertising agencies based in New York, London, Paris, and Tokyo.

Aware of the social dangers that such a state of affairs poses, Lasn issued a "Media Manifesto," in obvious parallelism with the many other manifestos that have been issued and that have "changed the world" (of which that of Marx and Engels is probably the most famous). The manifesto has five main resolutions that culture-jammers are determined to maintain:

- "We will take on the archetypal mind polluters—Marlboro, Budweiser, Benetton, Coke, McDonald's, Calvin Klein—and beat them at their own game."
- "We will uncool their billion dollar images with uncommercials on TV, subvertisements in magazines and anti-ads right next to theirs in the urban landscape."
- "We will take control of the role that the tobacco, alcohol, fashion, cosmetics, food and automobile corporations play in our lives. We will hold their marketing strategies up to public scrutiny and set new agendas in their industries."
- "We will culture jam the pop culture marketeers—MTV, Time Warner, Sony—and bring their image factories to a sudden, shuddering halt."
- "On the rubble of the old media culture, we will build a new one with a non-commercial heart and soul."

The various issues of *Adbusters*—a name evocative of both the "busting" of advertising and the title of the 1984 movie *Ghostbusters,* and thus also evoking the sense of the banishing, or even exorcism of the "ghosts" of capitalism—realizes the aims of the manifesto through subvertisements and articles. Subvertisements are ad texts that literally subvert the meanings of the brand messages in them. They take the signification systems of ad texts and turn them literally on their heads.

With all its good intentions, the culture-jamming and other anti-brand movements are hardly constructive ones, given that they really provide no alternatives to the way business is to be conducted in the Global Village. Theirs is a just and noble goal. Everyone is indeed appalled by images of poverty in the village and by the exploitation of the human and ecological resources that unbridled capitalism brings, as the many images in *Adbusters* constantly emphasize. Yet the belief of anti-brand individuals today is really no more than a modern-day version of anti-bourgeois sentiments expressed over the centuries in various forms and in political and social movements. The underlying assumption of all such movements is that bourgeois capitalism, in its relentless aim to guarantee profit (at any cost), is insensitive to basic human concerns, promoting an unbridled form of materialism that has affected societies negatively. Branding is considered to be a symptom of this fundamental bourgeois aim. But this is an ideological assumption, not a fact. One can argue, on the contrary, that the lifestyles crystallizing from democratic bourgeois capitalism have produced positive results that could never have been achieved under any other system. Something as seemingly banal as the widespread proliferation of cosmetics promoted by brand advertising has, as it turns out, had the kinds of positive outcomes that groups such as culture jammers would undoubtedly applaud (Peiss 1998). The mass production of cosmetics has had a definite impact in guiding the women's liberation movement, allowing them to express their sexuality openly—something that other kinds of political–social systems have tended to strictly forbid. The founders and early leaders of the "cosmetic movement" were women of low birth—Elizabeth Arden (1884–1966), a Canadian, was the daughter of poor tenant farmers, Helena Rubinstein (1870–1965), was born of poor Jewish parents in Poland, and Madam C. J. Walker (1867–1919) was born to former slaves in Louisiana. While it is true that cosmetic brand advertising has preyed on social fears associated with "bad complexions," "aging," etc., the cosmetic industry has at the same time allowed women to assert their sexuality, not conceal it.

As Heath and Potter (2004) have recently argued, the culture-jamming movement to create "brand-free" economics will not work because ultimately it constitutes nothing more than a way to promote no-brand and no-logo products. To emphasize their point, they refer to a 2003 *Adbusters* announcement that it would be selling its own brand of subversive shoe, the Blackspot Sneaker, to counteract the success of the Nike brand product. In effect, Heath and Potter argue, the Blackspot Sneaker ad employs the same kinds of advertising style as Nike. The irony of the whole exercise is that this very fact seems to have escaped the attention of culture jammers. Culture jamming turns out to be no more than an appealing form of self-deception. It is relevant to note that the culture jammers rarely go after the "small brands," just after the successful ones, defending the smaller and local brands against the "biggies" in the global marketplace. Moreover, an examination of the issues of *Adbusters* published up to 2005 does not show any subvertise-ments against brands that may be said to have "cultural content," such as bookstore companies and record labels of classical music or jazz. This suggests a rather selective and elitist view of branding, not a truly subversive one.

The same irony applies to other anti-brand groups. Take, for example, the vociferous "religious right" groups in the US, who are wont to blame the media and open sexual representations in advertisements for all that ails the country. Yet, as we have seen, the leaders of those very groups use advertising and the media to great advantage themselves, to purvey their ideas and their own products (videos, CDs, etc.) promising salvation and comfort to all their followers. Televangelism is a perfect example of how the very people who condemn the media use it for their own ends. In the 1988 election, one televangelist, Pat Robertson, even ran for president of the US with the full support of various media moguls, including Rupert Murdoch. Robertson's religious fundamentalism was well known, since he claimed to speak in tongues and have direct access to God.

A more rational approach to the branding movement today is the one taken by a San Francisco-based group that calls itself the Public Media Center (Hazen and Winokur 1997: 50–1), which is lobbying to make advertising more "honest," and less exploitive of younger minds, as Alissa Quart (2003) has also observed. The real problem with the branding process is that the critics and defenders of it are both right. The goal of capitalist systems is to promote a consumerist lifestyle, so that profits can be assured. To do so they base their business strategies on selling images and their meanings, rather than products in themselves. Day in and day out, the fragmented lifestyle images coming out of the media are bound to influence our overall view that reality is illusory and surreal, that human actions are a montage of disconnected images, desires, feelings, and that the only achievable goal of life is pleasure through consumption. It is also true, as media critics argue, that the messages of consumerism are modern-day surrogates for traditional forms of religious discourse, whose goal has always been the promulgation of the "good news." Today, the gospel, as Bachand (1992: 6) quips, "is being announced by advertisers." And we have, largely, become its converts. But within the same world it is possible to expose the banality of consumerism by using the same devices of the branding movement, as have the culture jammers. Therein lies the paradox of life today in the Global Village.

7

CONCLUSION

By way of conclusion, I would like to tie together some loose ends that I have attempted to weave throughout this book. One of my main goals has been to argue that brands have a strong emotional appeal because they are signs standing for *ideas* that have great emotional appeal. Like the icons of Byzantium they are perceived subconsciously as the means for attaining things that are beyond our reach. As Bedbury (2002: 14) aptly puts it, branding is a process that is "akin to alchemy." A coffee bean is really just a coffee bean until someone gives it a name, such as Starbucks, and then, like alchemical magic, it turns into a coffee experience served in a pleasant and chic environment known as a coffee house. Similarly, a sneaker is just a sneaker, until it is named Nike, at which point it becomes something deeper, inspirational, associated with the world of sports and fitness. Names such as Chanel No. 5, Audi's A4 and Mazda's RX-7 evoke numerological and mystical connotations. By imbuing products with hidden ancient symbolism, the marketer strategically re-creates our psychic past—a past in which symbols emerged as the elemental building-blocks of culture. Early symbolism was inextricably intertwined with an innate sense of mystery—a sense leading to the establishment of the ancient crafts of astrology and alchemy. The number 5, for example, was associated in ancient numerological systems to the pentagon and its mystical derivative the pentagram. The Pythagoreans ascribed the sagacity of womanhood to this five-sided figure—a symbol that blended the profane and sacred elements of life. This is likely the reason (conscious or unconscious) why the most powerful nation in the world has named and designed the headquarters of its defense system as "the Pentagon."

Marketers are keenly aware of the magic of symbols. The use of the number 7 in branding brings this out perfectly. This number has always been considered to have "magical" meanings—there are 7 days and 7 nights, 7 wonders of the world, 7 dwarfs, 7 deadly sins, 7 gods of good fortune in Japanese lore, and of course the soft drink 7-Up (pun intended). The list of the mystical meanings associated with the number 7 is a truly mind-boggling one. No wonder that so many products now incorporate the number 7 as part of their brand identity, from cars to soft drinks. The marketer's occultism works its unconscious magic on modern-day humans, making them see, for example, products as necessary for success or creating distinctions between better or worse— be it body shape, hairstyle, or brand of blue jeans. It is the symbolism of brands that creates allegiances to them. Their symbolic efficacy works its magic on every person in every society.

This would also explain why such items as Coca-Cola bottles, pet rocks, and other such apparently trivial artifacts are preserved by common people and why they now have historical value. As signs they are social constructs. Since their launch in 1959, the "Barbie" dolls, for instance, have become part of the experience of growing up for many little girls in the West. This is why Barbie has been consistently "updated" to keep in step with changing conceptions of female childhood. To wit, through the years she has taken on the roles of astronaut, athlete, ballerina, businesswoman, dancer, dentist, doctor, firefighter, paleontologist, police officer, lead singer of a rock band (Barbie and the Rocket's), and has even been a UNICEF volunteer. Mattel, the parent company that designs and manufactures the doll, even went so far as to provide Barbie with a "handsome boyfriend" named Ken. With his arrival, Barbie was raised to a new plateau, one that elevated her status and reaffirmed her as a true icon of contemporary popular culture.

McLuhan (1964) claimed that objects and tools are extensions of human anatomy and mentation. For instance, telescopes enable humans to see farther than their eyesight would otherwise permit; bicycles and cars extend the human foot; weapons are an extension of our hands, nails, and teeth; clocks our internal rhythms; houses our body's heat-control system; clothing our skin; the computer our central nervous system, etc. These extensions are real and tangible. This extensive pro-cess can be called, simply, "objectification." Branding is a contemporary version of objectification.

Yet brands have come to pervade contemporary social life in a fashion unimaginable in the past. Moreover, they have become the focus of anxieties about the way that we live in the industrialized West. The branded Global Village in which most of us live may, in actual fact, be shaping the world negatively, as culture jammers and others like them believe. And, admittedly, as denizens of the village we are tacitly allowing the image-makers to tell us what is important in life and that a worthwhile life can be measured in terms of how many material objects we get to own, and how many pleasures we get to feel. On the other hand, it is liberating to be in a village that is increasingly liberating itself of the authoritarian structures imposed by the hegemonic political systems of the past. At no other time in history has so much lifestyle choice been made available to so many as today. The answer to the dilemmas posed by life in the Global Village is, in my view, to become aware of the image-making strategies that are utilized to promote un-bridled materialism. In my opinion, the conceptual tools offered by semiotics make this realizable.

The Global Village is hardly Utopia. Some have even written it off as an anti-Utopian social order characterized by human misery and oppression. But Utopias are figments of the imagination. After all, the Global Village not only besieges us with brand images; it also provides the services and products that ultimately help the "common person" to survive longer than ever before; and, of course, it also provides the means to achieve a degree of affluence that has never been attained by so many at any other time in history.

While it is true that the Global Village has transformed the world into a consumerist one (at any cost), characterized by the poetic logic of brand management and the branding of culture, it is also true that constant changes are coming from within the village, making it unstable at best. Economics alone, as history informs us, cannot run a society forever. In the meanwhile, I cannot but conclude this book in agreement with the controversial writer Camille Paglia, who chastises those who wish to bring down the current capitalistic system, by pointing out simply that it is profoundly hypocritical of such intellectuals "to enjoy the pleasures and conveniences of capitalism, while sneering at it" (1991: 25).

REFERENCES

Allen, G. (2000) *Intertexuality*. London: Routledge.

Anderson, W. T. (1992) *Reality Isn't What It Used to Be*. San Francisco, CA: HarperCollins.

Andren, G. L., Ericsson, L., Ohlsson, R., and Tännsjö, T. (1978) *Rhetoric and Ideology in Advertising*. Stockholm: AB Grafiska.

Aronson, A. (2000) Reading Women's Magazines. *Media History* 6(2): 111–13.

Atkin, D. (2004) *The Culting of Brands*. New York: Portfolio.

Atwan, R. (1979) *Edsels, Luckies and Frigidaires: Advertising the American Way*. New York: Dell.

Bachand, D. (1992) The Art of (in) Advertising: From Poetry to Prophecy. *Marketing Signs* 13: 1–7.

Barthes, R. (1957) *Mythologies*. Paris: Seuil.

—— (1973) *Mythologies*. A. Lavers (trans.). London: Paladin.

—— (1977) *Image–Music–Text*. London: Fontana.

Baudrillard, J. (1973) *The Implosion of Meaning in the Media*. New York: Semiotexte Press.

—— (1978) *Toward a Critique of the Political Economy of the Sign*. St Louis, MO: Telos Press.

—— (1981) *For a Critique of the Political Economy of the Sign*. St Louis, MO: Telos Press.

—— (1988) *The Mirror of Production*. St Louis, MO: Telos Press.

—— (1998) *The Consumer Society*. London: Sage Publications.

Beard, A. (2001) *Texts and Contexts*. London: Routledge.

Beasley, R., Danesi, M., and Paul Perron, P. (2000) *Signs for Sale: An Outline of Semiotic Analysis for Advertisers and Marketers*. Ottawa: Legas Press.

Bedbury, S. (2002) *A Brand New World*. Harmondsworth: Penguin.

Berger, A. A. (2000) *Ads, Fads, and Consumer Culture: Advertising's Impact on American Character and Society*. Lanham MD: Rowman & Littlefield.
—— (2005) *Shop 'Til You Drop: Consumer Behavior and American Culture*. Lanham, MD: Rowman & Littlefield.
Bergin, T. G. and Fisch, M. (1984 [1948]) *The New Science of Giambattista Vico*. Ithaca, NY: Cornell University Press.
Bernardelli, A. (ed.) (1997) *The Concept of Intertextuality Thirty Years On: 1967–1997*. Special Issue of Versus, 77/78. Milano: Bompiani.
Bryman, A. (2004) *The Disneyization of Society*. London: Sage.
Cherry, C. (1957) *On Human Communication*. Cambridge, MA.: MIT Press.
Coupland, D. (1991) *Generation X*. New York: St Martin's.
Danesi, M. (1998) Gender Assignment, Markedness, and Indexicality: Results of a Pilot Study. *Semiotica* 121 (3/4): 213–39.
—— (2003) *Forever Young: The "Teen-Aging" of Modern Culture*. Toronto: University of Toronto Press.
Danziger, P. (2004) *Why People Buy Things They Don't Need: Understanding and Predicting Consumer Behavior*. Dearborn, MI: Dearborn Trade Publishing.
Davenport, G. (1984) *The Geography of the Imagination*. London: Picador.
Davies, W. V. (1988) *Egyptian Hieroglyphs*. Berkeley, CA: University of California Press.
Deely, J. (1994) *The Human Use of Signs, or Elements of Anthroposemiosis*. Lanham, MD: Rowman & Littlefield.
DeLong, M. R. and Bye, E. K. (1990) Apparel for the Senses: The Use and Meaning of Fragrances. *Journal of Popular Culture* 24(3): 81–8.
Driver, G. R. (1976) *Semitic Writing: From Pictograph to Alphabet*. London: Oxford University Press.
Drucker, J. (1995) *The Alphabetic Labyrinth: The Letters in History and Imagination*. London: Thames & Hudson.
Dyer, G. (1982) *Advertising as Communication*. London: Routledge.
Eco, U. (1979) *The Role of the Reader: Explorations in the Semiotics of Texts*. Bloomington, IN: Indiana University Press.
—— (1990) *The Limits of Interpretation*. Bloomington, IN: Indiana University Press.
Ewen, S. (1988) *All Consuming Images*. New York: Basic Books.
Frank, T. (1997) *The Conquest of Cool: Business Culture, Counterculture, and the Rise of Hip Consumerism*. Chicago: University of Chicago Press.
—— (2000) *One Market under God: Extreme Capitalism, Market Populism, and the End of Democracy*. New York: Anchor Books.
Freedman, J. L. (2002) *Media Violence and Its Effect on Aggression: Assessing the Scientific Evidence*. Toronto: University of Toronto Press.
Goddard, A. (1998) *The Language of Advertising*. London: Routledge.
Habermas, J. (1989) *The Structural Transformation of the Public Sphere: Inquiry into a Category of Bourgeois Society*, trans. T. Burger and P. Lawrence. Oxford: Polity.

Hays, C. (2004) *The Real Thing: Truth and Power at the Coca-Cola Company*. New York: Random House.

Hazen, D. and Winokur, J. (eds) (1997) *We the Media: A Citizen's Guide to Fighting for Media Democracy*. New York: The New Press.

Heath, J. and Potter, A. (2004) *The Rebel Sell: Why Culture Can't Be Jammed*. New York: HarperCollins.

Heggli, G. (1993) Talking with Readers: An Alternative Approach to Popular Literature. *Journal of Popular Culture* 26(4): 11–18.

Hermerén, L. (1999) *English for Sale: A Study of the Language of Advertising*. Lund: Lund University Press.

Hine, T. (1995) *The Total Package: The Secret History and Hidden Meanings of Boxes, Bottles, Cans, and Other Persuasive Containers*. Boston, MA: Little, Brown.

Hoffman, A. (1996) *Steal This Book*. New York: Four Walls, Eight Windows.

Holt, D. B. (2004) *How Brands Become Icons: the Principles of Cultural Branding*. Boston, MA: Harvard Business School Press.

Illich, I. and Sanders, B. (1988) *The Alphabetization of the Popular Mind*. San Francisco: North Point Press.

Karmen, S. (1989) *Through the Jungle: The Art and Business of Making Music for Commercials*. New York: Billboard Books.

Key, W. B. (1972) *Subliminal Seduction*. New York: Signet.

—— (1976) *Media Sexploitation*. New York: Signet.

—— (1980) *The Clam-Plate Orgy*. New York: Signet.

—— (1989) *The Age of Manipulation*. New York: Henry Holt.

Kilbourne, J. (1999) *Can't Buy My Love: How Advertising Changes the Way I Feel*. New York: Simon & Schuster.

Klein, N. (2000) *No Logo: Taking Aim at the Brand Bullies*. Toronto: Alfred A. Knopf.

Klein, R. (1993) *Cigarettes Are Sublime*. Durham, MD: Duke University Press.

Kress, G. (1996) *Reading Images: The Grammar of Visual Design*. London: Routledge.

Lasn, K. (2000) *Culture Jam: The Uncooling of America*. New York: Morrow.

Lindstrom, M. (2005) *Brand Sense: Build Powerful Brands through Touch, Taste, Smell, Sight, and Sound*. New York: Free Press.

Lotman, Y. (1991) *Universe of the Mind: A Semiotic Theory of Culture*. Bloomington, IN: Indiana University Press.

McLuhan, M. (1962) *The Gutenberg Galaxy*. Toronto: University of Toronto Press.

—— (1964) *Understanding Media*. London: Routledge & Kegan Paul.

Man, J. (2000) *Alpha Beta: How 26 Letters Shaped the Western World*. New York: John Wiley & Sons.

Mandoki, K. (2003) Point and Line over the Body: Social Imaginaries Underlying the Logic of Fashion. *Journal of Popular Culture* 36(3): 600–23.

Marks, S. (2005) *Finding Betty Crocker*. New York: Simon & Schuster.

Mick, D. G., Burroughs, J. E., Hetzel, P., and Brannen, M. Y. (2004) Pursuing the Meaning of Meaning in the Commercial World: An International Review of Marketing and Consumer Research Founded on Semiotics. *Semiotica* 152 (1/4): 1–74.

Munck, R. (2004) *Globalization and Social Exclusion*. Bloomfield, CT: Kumarian Press.

Myers, G. (1994) *Words in Ads*. London: Arnold.

Paglia, C. (1991) *Sexual Personae*. New York: Random House.

Panati, C. (1984) *Browser's Book of Beginnings*. Boston, MA: Houghton Mifflin.

Peirce, C. S. (1931–58) *Collected Papers of Charles Sanders Peirce*, Vols 1–8, C. Hartshorne and P. Weiss (eds). Cambridge, MA: Harvard University Press.

Peiss, K. (1998) *Hope in a Jar: The Making of America's Beauty Culture*. New York: Metropolitan Books.

Possamai, A. (2005) *Religion and Popular Culture: A Hyper-Real Testament*. New York: Peter Lang.

Quart, A. (2003) *Branded: The Buying and Selling of Teenagers*. New York: Basic Books.

Reichert, T. (2003) *The Erotic History of Advertising*. Amherst, NY: Prometheus Books.

Ries, A. and Ries, L. (2002) *The Fall of Advertising and the Rise of PR*. New York: HarperCollins.

Ritzer, G. (2004) *The McDonaldization of Society*. Thousand Oaks, CA: Pine Forge.

Roelcke, T. (2002) Efficiency of Communication: A New Concept of Language Economy. *Glottometrics* 4: 27–38.

Roy, M. (2000) *Sign after the X*. Vancouver: Advance Artspeak.

Saussure, F. de (1916) *Cours de linguistique générale*. Paris: Payot.

Schlosser, E. (2001) *Fast Food Nation*. Boston, MA: Houghton Mifflin.

Stevens, A. (1990) *On Jung*. London: Routledge.

Straubhaar, J. and LaRose, R. (2000) *Media Now: Communications Media in the Information Age*. Belmont, CA: Wadsworth.

Tash, M. (1979) Headlines in Advertising: The Semantics of Deviation. *Forum Linguisticum* 3: 222–41.

Twitchell, J. B. (2000) *Twenty Ads that Shook the World*. New York: Crown.

—— (2004) *Branded Nation*. New York: Simon & Schuster.

Underhill, P. (2004) *Call of the Mall*. New York: Simon & Schuster.

Wheeler, A. (2003) *Designing Brand Identity*. New York: John Wiley & Sons.

White, E. B. (1991) *Writings from the New Yorker 1927–1976*. New York: HarperCollins.

Williamson, J. (1996) But I Know What I Like: The Function of Art in Advertising, Paul Cobley (ed.), *The Communication Reader*. London: Routledge, pp. 396–402.

Wright, M. (1997) When Strength Means Death! *Brand Strategy*, 107 (December 12).

Zipf, G. K. (1935) *Psycho-Biology of Languages*. Boston, MA: Houghton-Mifflin.

—— (1949) *Human Behavior and the Principle of Least Effort*. Boston, MA: Addison-Wesley.

FURTHER READING

There are a number of useful books that deal with branded cultural trends, advertising, consumerism, and the effects of marketing on people and societies. Many of the volumes on the market are "How to" books that tend to have short shelf lives (these have been avoided here, but they are easy to track down, especially in business bookshops). There are also a few good books that introduce the kind of semiotic analysis which some brand management demands and which is certainly necessary for understanding message construction in branded commodities.

BRANDS AND THE BRANDING OF CULTURE

Aaker, D. A. (1991) *Managing Brand Equity: Capitalizing on the Value of a Brand*. New York: Jossey Bass Wiley.

> Oft-cited primer on how to establish and maintain brand equity. Undertakes rudimentary analysis of relations between slogans, straplines, and logos.

Aaker, D. A. (2002) *Building Strong Brands*. New York: Simon & Schuster.

> A kind of sequel to *Managing Brand Equity*. This time, Aaker focuses on various case histories, introducing the idea of brand-as-person, brand-as-organization, and brand-as-symbol.

Bedbury, S. (2002) *A New Brand World: 8 Principles for Achieving Brand Leadership in the 21st Century*. Harmondsworth: Penguin.

> A primer of brand management that attempts to provide "what it says on the tin."

Czerniawski, R. D. and Maloney, M. W. (1999) *Creating Brand Loyalty: The Management of Power Positioning and Really Great Advertising*. New York: Amacom.

This looks at the philosophy behind brands, rather than at the techniques of brand image-making in themselves and at the resulting meanings that these are designed to generate. The book constitutes a "look behind the scenes" at how brands are discussed and studied by marketers, as well as at the financial implications that branding entails.

Ford, K. (2005) *Brands Laid Bare: Using Market Research for Evidence-Based Brand Management*. New York: Wiley.

A book that is largely about the customer and his/her associations with brands. It shows how market research can produce information on customer needs and desires. Sections on "What do people want from a brand," brand equity, and segmentation.

Frank, T. (1997) *The Conquest of Cool*. Chicago: University of Chicago Press.

Frank, T. (2002) *One Market under God: Extreme Capitalism, Market Populism, and the End of Democracy*. New York: Anchor Books.

Both books present persuasive arguments that our branded culture is contradictory at best, and morally bankrupt at worst. Frank is particularly effective at putting holes into the myths that the new market populism is a solution to the problems that have beset capitalism in the past.

Hine, T. (1995) *The Total Package: The Secret History and Hidden Meanings of Boxes, Bottles, Cans, and Other Persuasive Containers*. Boston, MA: Little, Brown.

An excellent treatment of the role of design in the creation of brand image. It shows how today's marketers create packages, containers, etc. that make all the right promises, through signification systems that play on fears, needs, and the pleasure principle.

Holt, D. (2004) *How Brands Become Icons: The Principles of Cultural Branding*. Cambridge, MA: Harvard Business School Press.

Discusses the big brands from the perspective of an issue that is important for the present volume: the branding of culture.

Jones, J. P. (ed). (1999) *How to Use Advertising to Build Strong Brands*. London: Sage.

Professional treatment of how brands are devised and how they are marketed. There is more depth of knowledge of practice here than in some of the anti-brand books.

Klein, N. (2000) *No Logo: Taking Aim at the Brand Bullies*. New York: Knopf.

A coruscating critique of the entire power structure and complicit social mores behind our contemporary branded culture.

Miller, J. and Muir, D. (2004) *The Business of Brands*. New York: Wiley.

An influential book which is largely about the efficacy of brands for business. Contains a wealth of case studies.

Packard, V. (1957) *The Hidden Persuaders*. New York: McKay.

Perhaps the starting point to the anti-brand movement. Largely dealing with the subliminal effects of advertising, it is a book that is still relevant. Many of the phenomena that Packard discusses have not changed since the era in which the book was written. Packard's work inspired an outpouring of studies in the 1970s, 1980s, and 1990s, examining the effects of advertising on individuals and on society at large (some of which are listed in the cited works section below). Brand advertising has also been the target of numerous major analytical, critical, and technical investigations over the same time period. The implicit question that most of the studies have entertained, without answering it in any definitive fashion, is whether branding has become a force molding cultural mores and individual behaviors, or whether it constitutes no more than a "mirror" of deeper cultural tendencies within urbanized, contemporary societies.

Roberts, K. (2004) *Lovemarks: The Future Beyond Brands*. London: Powerhouse.

Somewhat speculative look at what a post-branding culture will entail. Looks at the trajectory of branding history and uses case studies from Saatchi accounts.

Wilmott, M. (2001) *Citizen Brands: Putting Society at the Heart of Your Business*. New York: John Wiley.

A response to Klein, although it does in no way undermine her basic argument that a branded culture makes for an "ethically lacking" world.

MARKETING SEMIOTICS

Floch, J.-M. (2000) (trans. A. McHoul and P. V. Osselger) *Visual Identities*. London: Continuum.

Six essays on various signs in commerce. Not always directly about specific brands, but a useful volume for its analyses of logos and other visual displays.

Floch, J.-M. (2001) (trans. R. O. Bodkin) *Semiotics, Marketing and Communication*. London: Palgrave.

Major book on "symbols for sale" and the "meaning" to be found in commercial life. Devoted to marketing in general, the volume nevertheless has indispensable insights that relate to the branding process.

Mick, D. G., Burroughs, J. E., Hetzel, P., and Brannen, M. Pursuing the meaning of meaning in the commercial world: an international review of marketing and consumer research founded on semiotics. *Semiotica* 152 (1/4): 1–74.

Many works have been written in the field of marketing semiotics. A substantive portion of these are reviewed in this comprehensive article. It is a technical review, but nevertheless highly readable.

Umiker-Sebeok, J. (ed.) (1988) *Marketing and Semiotics: New Directions in the Study of Signs for Sale*. Bloomington, IN: Indiana University Press.

A collection that has become a classic in a relatively short space of time. Contains various contributions, a number of which touch on brands.

SEMIOTIC ANALYSIS (GENERAL)

Cobley, P. (ed.) (2001) *The Routledge Companion to Semiotics and Linguistics*. London: Routledge.

Exactly what its title says it is—a textual "companion" that will allow the non-expert to grasp the relevance of semiotics beyond the terminological quagmire and, consequently, to penetrate the essence of what semiotics is all about. In addition to a dictionary of 200 basic entries, written in clear language by some of the leading semioticians and linguists in the world today, the *Companion* contains ten introductory essays, also written by experts in their respective fields, dealing with the main trends in theory, methodology, and practice. In effect, Cobley's volume is both a reference tool and a textbook introducing the fields of contemporary semiotics and linguistics to a broad audience.

Danesi, M. (1999) *Of Cigarettes, High Heels, and Other Interesting Things: An Introduction to Semiotics*. New York: St Martin's.

Written in a user-friendly style, my aim in this book is to present cultural semiotics to a large audience.

Eco, U. (1976) *A Theory of Semiotics*. Bloomington, IN: Indiana University Press.

Highly technical, but hugely influential theory of "how to do" semiotics.

Johansen, J. D. and Larsen, S. E. (2002) *Signs in Use: An Introduction to Semiotics*. London: Routledge.

An introduction to semiotics which is unusual—and valuable—because it considers the breadth of possibilities of semiotic analysis across culture *and* nature. Shows how everyday objects and facts have considerable semiotic potential.

Nöth, W. (1990) *Handbook of Semiotics*. Bloomington, IN: Indiana University Press.

As comprehensive a handbook on all areas of semiotics as one could wish for, despite its age. Contains a wealth of references to further reading.

Sebeok, T. A. (2001) *Signs: An Introduction to Semiotics*. Toronto: University of Toronto Press.

Much less technical than Eco, but nevertheless comprehensive in its overview of the diversity of signs.

van Leeuwen, T. (2005) *Introducing Social Semiotics*. London: Routledge.

An excellent introduction to "social semiotics" (the Anglo-Australian school, influenced by the linguist, Halliday), with a focus on advertising.

FURTHER RESOURCES

Note that website addresses are particularly transient and subject to change at short notice.

ACADEMIC JOURNALS

There are hundreds of journals on marketing, market research, business, and advertising. Many of them feature articles devoted to research on brands. The following is a short, selective list.

BrandLogic

> Online journal with special issues devoted to specific aspects of brands, brand equity, the branding of culture, and consumer behavior.

DMI Review

> A journal devoted to articles about design in organizations. Regularly features articles about brands.

International Journal of Research in Marketing (IJRM)

> General marketing theory (including brands). Invariably features papers on empirical research.

Journal of the Academy of Marketing Science

> Highly theoretical articles on marketing, but the journal often features articles on branding.

Journal of Advertising

> Major journal of advertising theory, regularly featuring articles about brand advertising.

Journal of Advertising Research

> Similarly stellar advertising journal with the focus on research.

Journal of Brand Management

> Not to be confused with the *Journal of Product and Brand Management*. This journal focuses on international brands, techniques used by agencies, theories of brand management, and approaches to brand equity.

Journal of Consumer Psychology

> Features papers from psychologists, but also contains a high proportion of papers on consumer behavior in relation to brands and commodities.

Journal of Consumer Research

> Articles on research into consumer behavior, some focusing on brands.

Journal of the Market Research Society

> Features articles on topics of value to market research, frequently about brands and brand equity.

Journal of Product and Brand Management

> Articles focus on issues that are to be taken into account when determining brand and pricing strategies and policies.

Marketing Science

> Features articles on empirical, usually quantitative, market research, often on brands.

MAGAZINES AND PERIODICALS

There are numerous magazines and periodicals on marketing, advertising, brand management, and market research. The following are a few of the most well-known.

Adbusters

> The well-known critical/satirical publication. Available at: www.adbusters.org/home/

AdMap

> Monthly. General magazine on advertising, marketing, and design. Available at: www.admapmagazine.com/

Advertising Age

> Weekly. American magazine, similar to *Campaign* (see below). Available at: www.adage.com/

Brand Strategy

Monthly. Contains news about new brands and strategies as well as think pieces on the nature of brands and how to research them. Available at: www.centaur.co.uk/communities/marketing/bs/default.aspx

Campaign

Weekly. Carries all the latest news from marketing and advertising. Available at: www.brandrepublic.com/magazines/campaign/index.cfm

Marketing

Weekly. Much more focused on marketing than on the world of advertising, in contrast to its sister publication, *Campaign* (see above). Regularly features special focus on brands. Available at: www.brandrepublic.com/magazines/marketing/

Marketing Management

Bi-monthly. The magazine of the American Marketing Association. Deals with issues of marketing strategy, including brand management. Available at: www.marketingpower.com/

Marketing Week

Weekly. News, comment, and analysis on new products and on brand strategies. Competitor to *Marketing* (see above). Available at: www.centaursubs.co.uk/

ONLINE RESOURCES

I counted over 6,000 websites dealing with semiotics and branding, logo, design, and advertising in early 2005. These range from brand advisors such The Institute of Brand Logic, Innsbruck (Conradstrasse 5–6020 Innsbruck, Austria), available at: www.institute-brandlogic.com/ and Semiotic Solutions, available at: www.semioticsolutions.com to culture-jamming websites (see info@adbusters.org and www.culturejammers.com). *Adbusters* offers a website and paper magazine with many clever parodies of major advertising campaigns and articles helping common people to recognize media manipulation. The magazine also provides information on lawsuits and legislation on consumer issues, links to send e-mail to big businesses about their marketing strategies, and other such matters.

Another good online source of information on brands apart from magazines are professional societies such as the Market Research Society, available at: www.mrs.org.uk or the advertising research foundation, available at: www.arfsite.org.

Use search engines to discover the sites of branding advisers and professional associations. Although they are often devoted to a "how to" approach to brands and are not informed by theory, semiotic or otherwise, they can usually tell you a great deal about how brands are constructed and the associations which accrue to certain brands.

INDEX

Related titles in this series

News

Jackie Harrison

From an author highly knowledgeable in the field, *News* is a handy
and accessible guide that examines the history of news, both as
newspapers and radio, and as entertainment and information, and
introduces students to the key concepts and issues that surround
the news.

Using up-to-date case examples such as the Hutton Report and
embedded journalists, from across a range of media including print,
radio, television and the internet, Jackie Harrison explains the
different theoretical approaches that have been used to study the
news, as well as providing an accessible introduction to how news
is produced and regulated, what counts as news, and how it is
selected and presented.

Topics covered include:

- introduction to the concept of news
- the growth and development of news
- technology, concentration and competition
- balancing freedom and responisibility
- regulatory control of the news
- making the news.

Written in a clear and lively style, *News* is the ideal introductory
book for students of media, communication and journalism.

ISBN10: 0–415–31949–8 (hbk)
ISBN10: 0–415–31950–1 (pbk)

ISBN13: 978–0–415–31949–2 (hbk)
ISBN13: 978–0–415–31950–8 (pbk)

Available at all good bookshops
For ordering and further information please visit:
www.routledge.com

Related titles in this series

Youth Media

Bill Osgerby

From the days of diners, drive-ins and jukeboxes, to today's world of iPods and the internet, *Youth Media* examines youth media in its economic, cultural and political contexts and explores:

- youth culture and the media
- the 'Fab Phenomenon': markets, money and media
- generation and degeneration in the media: representations, responses and 'effects'
- media, subculture and lifestyle
- global media, youth culture and identity
- youth and new media.

Analyzing the nature of different forms of communication as well as reviewing their production and consumption, this is an essential introduction to this key area in communication and cultural studies.

ISBN10: 0–415–23807–2 (hbk)
ISBN10: 0–415–23808–0 (pbk)

ISBN13: 978–0–415–23807–6 (hbk)
ISBN13: 978–0–415–23808–3 (pbk)

Available at all good bookshops
For ordering and further information please visit:
www.routledge.com

Related titles from Routledge

Performing Consumers: Global Capital and its Theatrical Seductions

Maurya Wickstrom

'Linking performance and global capitalism, Wickstrom offers a brilliant analysis of the miasma of "the market." I could not put the book down.'

Elinor Fuchs, *Yale School of Drama*

Performing Consumers is a searching exploration of the way in which brands insinuate themselves into the lives of ordinary people who encounter them at branded superstores.

Looking at our performative desire to "try on" otherness, Maurya Wickstrom employs five American brandscapes to serve as case studies: Ralph Lauren; Niketown; American Girl Place; Disney store and *The Lion King*; and The Forum Shops at Caesar's Palace in Las Vegas. In this post-product era, each builds for the performer/consumer an intensely pleasurable, somatic experience of merging into the brand and reappearing as the brand, or the brand's fictional meanings.

To understand this embodiment as the way that capital is producing subjectivity as an aspect of itself, Wickstrom casts a wide net, drawing on:

* the history of capital's relationship with theatre;
* political developments in the United States; and
* recent work in political science, philosophy, and performance studies.

An adventurous study of theatrical indeterminancy and material culture, *Performing Consumers* brilliantly takes corporate culture to task.

ISBN10: 0–415–33944–8 (hbk)
ISBN10: 0–415–33945–6 (pbk)
ISBN13: 978–0–415–33944–5 (hbk)
ISBN13: 978–0–415–33945–2 (pbk)

Available at all good bookshops
For ordering and further information please visit:
www.routledge.com